# THE WAY **BACK TO HOPE**

## The Truth about
## Overcoming Disappointment

# Praise for *The Way Back to Hope*

Finding our way back to joy and hope is a lifelong learning process. We have all had our own "most trying season." These seasons are often the greatest challenge we face. Amy Calkins has written a book from her own deep well of soul-searching, experience, and finding understanding. I appreciate what she has written in *The Way Back to Hope*. If you have found yourself living past your ability to see hope because the pain and chaos have taken over, please let me encourage you to allow someone who has been there to hand you a map in this journey. This book will help you find real, helpful goals and bypass the many lies that hinder and hurt us when we are weak and discouraged. I highly recommend *The Way Back to Hope* as a direction-finding tool in the journey of plowing through the fog of war and allowing God to set your feet on the rock of hope.

—**Danny Silk**, President of Life Academy;
author of *Keep Your Love On* and *Loving Our Kids on Purpose*

This book is really refreshing! Amy tackles the reality that the Church has talked a lot about victory without being honest about how desperately hard the Christian journey can be. She deals with real life struggles and the emotions that accompany them, as well as the story of how God healed her heart—"not by giving her answers, but by giving her hope." She helps us understand how pain alerts us to the real problem—the wounds in our hearts that come from unresolved disappointment. Instead of telling people that their pain is a result of God's will for their lives, she encourages us to tell them the truth: that God grieves with them. Amy candidly writes from her own experience to help us understand how we can live free of offense in the middle of the unknown. She encourages us to grieve and invite God into the journey with us. The truths found in this book will lead you into the kind of hope that will not only cause you to weather the storms, but also access heaven's solutions for them. I highly recommend this book!

—**Larry Kreider**, International Director of DOVE International;
author of more than forty books

The need to overcome disappointment is very current and prevalent in the Christian world. This can include disappointment from personal challenges, betrayals, and the failures of leaders we have positioned ourselves to receive from. The responsibility to overcome disappointment will always be our own. We have choices to make, and Amy walks us through the journey of overcoming lies, making healthy heart choices, and discovering true biblical hope in the midst of things we cannot understand or solve in our own strength. It is my pleasure to endorse this book, this roadmap to hope. I commend it as a manual to help people navigate disappointment, but also as a study guide for a small group before disappointment invades our lives. This book will keep your hope alive and, consequently, keep your soul healthy.

—**Paul Manwaring**, Senior Leadership Team, Bethel Church Redding;
author of *What on Earth is Glory*, *Kisses from a Good God*, and *Things Fathers Do*

In *The Way Back to Hope*, Amy Calkins will inspire and equip you to be tenacious and wise in overcoming the obstacles and challenges that would tempt you to stop having big dreams for your life. She shares many of her challenging life experiences in which she persevered and found her own way back to hope. I frequently say, "There are no hopeless circumstances, only people who do not have hope," and this book is an example of what it looks like to find hope in every circumstance. Thank you, Amy, for being a strong and effective voice of hope in this hour. Those who read this book will be glad they did.

—**Steve Backlund**, Founder of Igniting Hope Ministries

*The Way Back to Hope* by Amy Calkins is an accessible, raw, and revelatory read into the journey of walking through the disappointments of life specifically in loss, grief, and recovery from trauma. Amy opens her soul to help us see ourselves in the doubts, questions, and physical and mental exhaustion of living in pain. She guides us through the scriptures into the revelation of the God who is there and willing to bring healing and restoration of hope, no matter how much the trauma of life has brought devastation. Her transparency is refreshing. Reading this book will bring healing and restoration to your soul.

—**Dr. Mike Hutchings**, Director of Education at Global Awakening; President of God Heals PTSD Foundation

All of us deal with pain and disappointment in life, but many of us don't know how to process it or how to turn our lives around when the seas get rough. Amy Calkins' book, *The Way Back to Hope,* offers keys to breakthrough through biblically understanding the problem of pain, God's will in the middle of the storm, and how to tackle the *why* questions that leave us paralyzed. I highly recommend this book as a resource for navigating painful issues in life and how we can all take courage to move forward into calmer waters of hope.

—**Theresa Dedmon**, Pastor and Director of Create Academy; author of *Created To Overcome* and *Born to Create*

*The Way Back to Hope* is one of the most candid, transparent, effective, and important books of our day to help one discover lasting freedom and hope. No one in life escapes pain. However, like a masterful surgeon, Amy digs to the innermost depths (and layers) of the misconceptions we often believe about God, ourselves, and the disappointments that life brings. When all is stripped away, what we find— in its purest form—is truth and healing. Few writers could capture and craft, as brilliantly as Amy has, the journey that touches us all at such a deep level. You will not only be personally and profoundly impacted by this book; you will be set free!

—**Anna Kramer**, Founder/Chief Creative Officer at Pneuma33 Creative; Founder/Editor in Chief of *World Changer Magazine*

We all experience hurt and grief in life. Most often, we try to push it down and push forward. As Amy shares in this book, it doesn't help to deny or ignore what we feel. Being very transparent about her own journey through pain, Amy provides practical and encouraging help in finding healing and returning to a place of hope again. It's a good read with biblical insight that I found very helpful.

—**Dr. Barry Wissler**, President of HarvestNet International

*The Way Back to Hope* is a wonderful book that reads like a conversation with a friend. It is consistently honest and persistently hope-filled. The pacing of the story-telling is clear and compelling. This book was not written in a vacuum, but was forged in the throes of real life traumas. I wept at times as Amy clearly communicated her pain through the process. Her revelations don't feel preachy. She simply reveals her heart as she encountered the Father's heart. She invites us into her thought processes as she ponders the counsel of the Lord. Speaking of pain and hope at the same time is a tricky pathway. Acknowledging the presence of suffering in trials can be taboo in some church cultures—often misjudged as a lack of faith. Amy's hope-filled honesty provides a safe place for readers to process their pain and experience their own unique healing in God's presence. Amy provides no easy formulas to "fix" us, instead pointing the way to His healing heart. This book will bring healing and hope to many. Thank you, Amy, for spending yourself to write it!

—**Dr. Dave Hess**, Co-Senior Leader, alongside his wife Sheri, of Christ Community Church, Camp Hill, PA; author of *Hope Beyond Reason* and *Side by Side*

Are you facing disappointment, pain, questions about God's will, or simply trying to understand *why* God has allowed something in your life? The temptation will be to stay stuck in the mire of hopelessness, but there is a way forward. Amy Calkins shares candid examples from her own experience and compelling insights into scripture and offers all of us a pathway back to hope. If you want practical ways to have your hope restored, then I highly recommend *The Way Back to Hope*.

—**Jimmy Nimon**, Lead Pastor of Lifeway Church, Lebanon, PA

In this book, my dear and talented friend, Amy, opens her heart about how she rediscovered hope. Amy's story will grip you as she shares how to find your way through disappointment to a hope only God can give. This book will encourage and strengthen you as you walk through difficulties, and it will set you on a new journey into *The Way Back to Hope*. Thank you, Amy. This is a must read!

—**Margie Fleurant**, Founder of Margie Fleurant Ministries; author of *Encountering God Through Prayer* and *Focus*

One of our greatest challenges as believers is to allow pain to draw us into deeper intimacy with Jesus instead of pushing Him away. In *The Way Back to Hope,* Amy does a beautiful job of laying out the journey of pain and how we, as believers in Jesus, can live in both pain and hope. With beautiful and heart-wrenching stories from her own journey through pain and disappointment, Amy points to a hope that can be found in the midst. She uncovers truth in the word of God and sets straight lies we have believed. I pray that as you read this book the truth will wash over you, and in the middle of your dark valley you will find that not only does God care, but He is right there with you, able to identify with your grief and pain. As you hold mystery in your heart, a deep joy and unending hope will become an anchor to your spirit.

—**Renée Evans**, Senior Pastor, Bethel Austin

Grief. Loss. Pain. Disappointment. How we process these seasons dramatically impacts our relationship with God and our destiny. *The Way Back to Hope* is a powerful book with a needed message. Amy Calkins skillfully leads us on a journey through the valley of the shadow of death. Using personal stories and biblical examples, she addresses common pitfalls in navigating disappointment and leads us through to healing and hope restored. This book will bring clarity to your circumstances, freedom to your emotions, and healing balm to your soul!

—**Jake Kail**, Apostolic Leader of Threshold Church, Lancaster, PA; author of *Setting Captives Free*

*The Way Back to Hope*—it sounds like a road map, and essentially it is! The hard fact about life is that each of us will face hurt and disappointment. The question is, how will we come through that hurt to a place of healing, wholeness, and hope? Amy's willingness to do the hard work of processing her own disappointments with God, others, and herself from a biblical perspective now provides a guide for others to do the same and return to a life of hope and faith. Thanks, Amy, for leading the way for many to follow! I am confident that God will use the words of this book to provide healing for many!

—**Kevin Eshleman**, Lead Pastor of Ephrata Community Church, Ephrata, PA

# THE WAY **BACK TO HOPE**

## The Truth about Overcoming Disappointment

AMY CALKINS

Songbird
BOOKS

Scripture quotations are taken from the New American Standard Bible®, Copyright © 1960, 1971, 1977, 1995 by the Lockman Foundation. All rights reserved. Emphasis within Scripture quotations is the author's own.

The poem "Small Boat" was originally published under the author's maiden name, Amy Good, in the anthology *Becoming Fire,* edited by Alexander Levering Kern (Andover-Newton Theological School, 2006).

Songbird Books
Ephrata, PA
amycalkins.com

Logo Design: Lauren Grisafi

Cover Photo: Irina Krutova on Unsplash

Layout and Cover Design: James Woosley, FreeAgentPress.com

ISBN: 979-8-9865045-0-6 (paperback)
ISBN: 979-8-9865045-1-3 (hardback)
ISBN: 979-8-9865045-2-0 (ebook)

*for Mark, Abigail, Evan, Susanna, & Annabelle*

*for all who have walked in the valley of the shadow of death*

# CONTENTS

## ACKNOWLEDGMENTS

Mark—for always loving and believing in me and for telling me my voice matters.

Abigail, Evan, Susanna, & Annabelle—for being my people, for welcoming me into your hearts and your journeys, and for letting me spend so many afternoons working on this project.

Mom & Dad—for your support and encouragement always and for your helpful feedback on the book.

Steve & Kathy Calkins—for believing in me and rejoicing with me.

Dr. Flora Armetta, Renee Groff, Brad Herman, Dr. Dave Hess, Katie Horst, Alicia Martin, Amber Porter, Dr. Kara Sensenig, Dr. Barry Wissler—for reading my first draft and giving me such helpful and encouraging feedback and also for being leaders and friends who are dear to my heart. Knowing each of you has changed me, and I am forever thankful for you.

Anna Elkins Sandeen—for your content editing prowess and also for being a friend and a poetic encourager.

Alicia Marshall—for your expert line editing and proofreading and for making time on top of your already busy life.

Brad Herman & Anna Kramer—for your support and feedback related to design and marketing. I would have been lost without you.

Jimmy & Lydia, Jake & Anna, Barry & Cheryl—for your friendship and the ways you supported our family during our darkest season. It means everything to me.

Jenna—for being an answer to prayer.

# INTRODUCTION

THIS BOOK IS NOT about my life, but it does tell part of my story—the part where I came face-to-face with crippling disappointment and loss and found my way through. I am not here to give you good Christian answers or five-step solutions, but to validate your experiences and pain, to question some unhelpful (and unbiblical) theology, and to show you the way back to hope.

For too long the Church has talked a lot about victory without being honest about how desperately hard the Christian journey can be. But if our victory is built on the foundation of dismissing or refusing to acknowledge our real-life struggles and the emotions that accompany them, we will find ourselves on shaky ground. Such victory has a hard time holding itself together. Jesus never runs from the hard stuff; he isn't afraid of the mess. He gets down in the dirt with us. He knows how to heal our hearts so they can become the foundation for true victory.

I first preached the message of this book in the Fall of 2017. At the time, my husband, Mark, and I were pastoring a church we had planted. After a few years of growing pains, we were finally gaining momentum. We had moved from meeting in a home to renting a hotel space. The presence of God showed up in powerful ways, and people's lives were changing. It felt like we were on the cusp of the breakthrough we had been praying and believing for. What I didn't know was that we were just a few months away from the beginning of the end of our vision.

That morning, as I preached on overcoming disappointment, my primary example from my life came from my on-going struggle with severe nerve pain in my arms and wrists. That continues to be a battle I fight, but it has paled in comparison to the pain of the disappointments and losses Mark and I have faced since.

In early 2018, our church leadership faced several significant challenges that led to fracturing within the church body. The momentum shifted, and people began leaving. By the end of that year, we were back to "starting over" numbers, and our hearts were weary. We wrestled with how to move forward.

Around that same time, we discovered that a close friend (someone I'd written and edited many books for over the last nine years) was living a duplicitous and predatory life. It was devastating. Realizing someone I had trusted implicitly had been using my writing gift to build credibility with those he was grooming shook me deeply.

Then, something terrible happened to one of our daughters. It's a story I cannot share publicly, but it was the worst experience of our lives. The trauma was such that we knew, for our family's sake, it was time to start over. In the spring of 2019, we passed the leadership of our church on to our associate leaders, Mark found a sales job, and we moved to a town about an hour away.

Of course, relocating didn't take away the pain of our losses or the grief associated with injustice, trauma, and betrayal. The next year would be our most intense year yet—as we walked with our daughter through her healing process, while also trying to embrace our own healing and find connection in a new place. Only a few years after I'd first felt God put this message on my heart, I found myself wrestling with disappointment and loss like never before.

In this book, I share my journey of overcoming disappointment and finding the way back to hope. While I do refer to some aspects of mental health as part of my journey, the purpose of this book does not encompass serious mental health struggles, and I do not consider myself qualified to address that topic. Instead, I seek to offer biblical hope and strategies for the mental and emotional struggles we all face during times of loss and disappointment. Often, these strategies can be enhanced through pastoral counseling and professional therapy.

Welcome to the story of how God healed my heart—not by giving me answers, but by giving me hope.

## Small Boat

On land it felt more solid, barely shook
against the tip of sea. The planks stuck hard
in sand, like forests settling down, the look
of certainty. We set out, cupped in wood
that pumped unsteady surf under my step.
I found, by the teacher, the safest seat.
But it was like the corners meant to keep
the earth taut had been loosened, like a sheet
that held no tension, sliding out below
me, and I knew we'd die. The waves rocked high
and stuttered. Still Jesus slept. And no
one understood how he could frown or why
he named our fear so strongly, calling out
to still the wind and shatter all our doubt.

# CHAPTER 1

# Disappointment at the Door

NONE OF US LOOK for disappointment. When we're young, many of us believe we will elude the disappointments our parents faced. We run forward with relentless optimism, believing our dreams will really happen, and everything will turn out well in the end. We know we may face a few bumps in the road, but we expect to traverse them safely.

And then life happens. At some point, each one of us finds ourselves face-to-face with disappointment, and we have to choose how to respond. The death of someone we love, the loss of a job, a divorce, an alienated child, an addiction, a betrayal, abuse, trauma, the death of a dream, a life-changing sickness or injury, miscarriage, infertility, an area of lack, a personal failure, unanswered prayers—many roads can lead to disappointment. Some of those disappointments are massive and life-altering; others seem smaller, but their emotional impact can be equally significant.

Ultimately, disappointment stems from the realization that life might not (or definitely will not) turn out how we hoped it would and the struggle to mentally and emotionally cope with that reality. When life punches a hole in our optimism, the deflation of our dreams leads to disappointment.

Years ago, before we moved across the country to California, we asked a group of friends to pray over us and send us into our next season. During that time, one friend felt like she heard God telling her that my writing and editing business would prosper greatly in the next season and that God would open incredible doors for me. Initially, this word came true. Without much effort on my part, doors began opening, and I found myself with almost more work than I could handle. Not only that, but I was working for authors I deeply respected. Their messages mattered to me, and I felt fulfilled using my talents to help spread their teachings.

Then, about a year into our time there, just as I was finishing my most exciting project to date, someone I had counted as a friend and colleague betrayed me. I'd been helping her, on a volunteer basis, to build her publishing company, so we met often. One day, she called me into her office. She told me she thought my writing abilities were lacking and revealed that she had criticized my work to several of my clients—people who also happened to be leaders at the church we both attended.

I was stunned.

In the moment, I could hardly speak. I had never imagined something like this could happen. She said her seemingly mean-spirited actions were inspired by a reluctant but justified obedience to her sense of duty and truth-telling. But I had so many questions. Why hadn't she told me first and offered to help me grow if she thought my work was lacking? Why had she acted in ways that seemed so pointedly malicious? How could she feel so calmly justified in doing this after I'd given hours of my time investing in her new company? Neither my brain nor my heart could comprehend it. Afterward, I climbed into my car and sobbed the whole way home.

In the months following, I found myself feeling deeply disappointed on multiple levels. I'd been betrayed by a friend, I'd lost work, I'd lost relationships, and I was face-to-face with the harshest criticism of my writing I'd ever received.

I recalled the prophetic word I'd received, and I wondered why it had initially come true, but then ultimately turned out to be the opposite. Why hadn't God come through for me like I thought he'd promised? I felt disappointed with myself, too. I wished I had made different decisions, but of course, when I made them, I had no idea what was around the corner. Most of all, I wondered whether I was fooling myself into thinking I was a better writer than I really was. This was a big and scary question that not only undermined my business, but also my personal writing dreams.

I had gone to California with stars in my eyes, but I left brokenhearted. When I least expected it, disappointment came knocking at my door, snickering at my dreams, telling me, "Welcome to reality." In this area of my life, I found myself echoing the sentiments of Naomi when all her hope seemed gone.

> But Naomi said, "Return, my daughters. Why should you go with me? Have I yet sons in my womb, that they may be your husbands? Return, my daughters! Go, for I am too old to have a husband. If I said I have hope, if I should even have a husband tonight and also bear sons, would you therefore wait until they were grown? Would you therefore refrain from marrying? No, my daughters; for it is harder for me than for you, for the hand of the Lord has gone forth against me" (Ruth 1:11–13).

The death of Naomi's husband and sons had seemed like a forever end to her hope of happiness—her hope of a family and heirs. In despair, she sent her daughters-in-law away, yet Ruth refused to leave and instead bound herself to her as a daughter. Though Naomi had been ready to give up, Ruth wouldn't let her. Together, they found a new life. The losses they had experienced were deep, yet they found a way to hope again. Neither of them knew it, but Boaz was waiting on the other side of their decision to say *no* to disappointment.

\*\*\*

None of us is lucky enough to avoid disappointment in this life. The question is, when we meet disappointment, will we let it through the door, listen to its mollifying words, invite it to stay? Or will we slam the door in its face?

It is so easy to listen to and agree with disappointment, because it seems to make sense. It appeals to our logic and tells us to judge life and others and even God by the fairness of our circumstances. But disappointment is ultimately a liar. It may make some good points, but its judgment is flawed. If we listen to it long enough, we end up in despair, joyless and sick in heart.

We end up like the dry bones in the prophet Ezekiel's vision. The Israelites had lost hope and fallen into despair, but God gave Ezekiel a vision of a valley full of dry bones, and he told Ezekiel to prophesy life into them. As Ezekiel prophesied to the bones, they began to rattle and come together into skeletons. Muscles and sinews formed; skin grew. But the bodies still had no breath, no life in them. So God told Ezekiel to prophesy again, saying "Come from the four winds, O breath, and breathe on these slain, that they come to life" (Ezek. 37:9). When he did, the breath of God entered the bodies, and they "stood on their feet, an exceedingly great army" (Ezek. 37:10). God then explained the vision to Ezekiel, saying:

> These bones are the whole house of Israel; behold, they say, "Our bones are dried up and our hope has perished. We are completely cut off." Therefore prophesy and say to them, "Thus says the Lord God, 'Behold, I will open your graves and cause you to come up out of your graves, My people...'" (Ezekiel 37:11–12).

What could be more hopeless than dry bones? But even dry, lifeless bones are not beyond hope in God's eyes. In him, the dry bones of disappointment and loss in our lives can stand up and become an exceedingly great army.

Despair is no one's destiny. Even when life looks like a valley of dry bones, God declares new life and new hope. He is not content to leave us in the graves of despair and disappointment. We were not made to live with sick hearts or broken hope. The potential of a mighty warrior still rattles in our bones. When we face disappointment, we have a choice.

Proverbs 13:12 says, "Hope deferred makes the heart sick, but desire fulfilled is a tree of life." For a time, I believed this verse meant that desires fulfilled are the key to happiness. But after I had tasted a few disappointments, this verse started to feel like a prison sentence rather than a promise. *What if my desires are never fulfilled? Am I relegated to the land of sick hearts?* Of course, in light of the cross, such an idea doesn't make much sense. In God's economy, he provides for thriving hearts, no matter our circumstances. I began to understand that this verse is descriptive, not prescriptive. It describes how life often works, not how it *should* work.

This is good news. It means we don't have to have sick hearts when things don't work out how we wanted—when God doesn't seem to come through like he promised. It means I could walk out of the disappointments of California still believing in dreams-come-true. I could forgive and let go, trusting in the God who can breathe life into dead bones, "who gives life to the dead and calls into being that which does not exist" (Rom. 4:17).

That is what Abraham, the father of faith, did—"in hope against hope, he believed, so that he might become a father of many nations according to that which had been spoken" (Rom. 4:18; see Gen. 15:1–6). Though all the signs pointed to his hope of a son being forever deferred, Abraham clung to the promise, and because of his unrelenting faith, he was counted as righteous (see Rom. 4:19–22). This story calls out to me in the seasons of hope deferred, reminding me that I don't have to give up. I don't have to stop believing. I don't have to become sick in heart.

Abraham and Sarah's story also comforts me, because their faith wasn't perfect. Abraham isn't called the father of faith because he never doubted. After all, the Bible tells us he had at least one season of doubt, when he thought he would help God out with his promise of a son by impregnating Sarah's maid, Hagar (see Gen. 16:1–5). When God came to Abraham to renew his promise to him, even after the episode with Hagar, Abraham laughed and said, "Will a child be born to a man one hundred years old? And will Sarah, who is ninety years old, bear a child?… Oh that Ishmael [Hagar's son] might live before You" (Gen. 17:17–18).

Here we find Abraham not only doubting the promise, but also wishing that God would just work the promise out in Abraham's way. Sarah also laughed at God's promise when the angels visited and declared that she would have a son within the next year (see Gen. 18:9–15). Abraham and Sarah were only one year away from the birth of their son Isaac, but neither one of them seemed to be exhibiting great faith. Abraham was still trying to fix up a solution for God. And both of them laughed at the possibility of pregnancy at their age.

Yet, when Hebrews 11—the great faith chapter—talks about Abraham and Sarah, we get a different story. "By faith, even Sarah herself received ability to conceive, even beyond the proper time of life, since she considered Him faithful who had promised" (Heb. 11:11). And the apostle Paul wrote about Abraham:

> Without becoming weak in faith he contemplated his own body, now as good as dead since he was about a hundred years old, and the deadness of Sarah's womb; yet, with respect to the promise of God, he did not waver in unbelief but grew strong in faith, giving glory to God, and being fully assured that what God had promised, He was able also to perform (Romans 4:19–21).

What this tells me is that God counted their faith as worthy even though it wasn't perfect. Even when they struggled to believe in their hearts, they still chose to believe. They still pointed their lives toward God, saying *yes* to his plan and trusting in his promises *even while* they wrestled with the whispers of disappointment and doubt about how it could be possible.

I think many of us can relate to this picture of faith. I'm glad the father of faith had his moments of struggle and that God still counted him as righteous because of his faith.

This divergence in the biblical accounts of Abraham and Sarah shows us that God really does accept faith as small as a mustard seed (see Matt. 17:20)—and that when he looks back on our journey, he sees it through the lens of our successes, not our failures. God knows Abraham and Sarah laughed, but he remembers them as those who believed the unbelievable and did not give up.

Abraham and Sarah weren't perfect, but against all odds, they didn't listen to disappointment. They didn't give up.

We don't have to either.

\*\*\*

Of course, saying "I don't have to give up" is simpler than living it. Turning down disappointment is not easy. Too many Christians act as though reciting Bible verses and doing all the right spiritual activities will magically make disappointment and pain go away. Like you can wake up one day and everything is just better. I am sure that has been true for some people, and I am also sure that it has not been true for many others.

Jesus is a miracle-worker, the God of the breakthrough. But his miracles aren't magic formulas. His work in our lives is always in partnership with our faith—faith that is both a gift and a journey. Trust, hope, peace—the inner workings of the Spirit—grow in our hearts over time. Jesus never offered to fix all our problems, but he does offer to go with us on the journey. Real life with Jesus takes real inner work. This work is, of course, empowered by his grace, but it's still intentional and purposeful and sometimes very hard. Saying that doesn't diminish the miracle of Christ's power in our lives.

It's been three years since Mark and I stepped down as pastors of the church we planted. Three years since we buried that dream. Three years since Mark left doing what he loves. We did it for a good reason—for the sake of one of our daughters, who had been through the unimaginable and needed a space to heal. But that didn't make it easier to lose our dream, to walk away from the vision and people we had so deeply loved and invested in. It has taken us three years (and counting) to sort through the layers of this loss. God has done miracles in our hearts and accelerated our process, yet it has still been a process. Every step of the healing journey has been an intentional choice. And every step has required courage.

For several months after we moved, I found myself feeling continually weary with the grief of what we'd walked through—the loss of the church, the losses in our daughter's life, the loss of friends and community. Starting over in a new community and making new friends is hard under normal circumstances. In the middle of grief, it felt impossible. It took everything in me to get out of bed every day, to keep up with my household responsibilities. The simplest things, like making breakfast or folding laundry, felt intolerably hard. I remember lying on my bed one afternoon and feeling like I just wanted to give up. My chest ached. It took so much effort to move. And I felt terribly alone. Who could possibly understand the complexity of what we'd been through?

Outside my window, the sky was brilliant, golden and blue and shimmery. I love to soak up a beautiful sky. It is one of my simple pleasures. But that day, as I looked impassively from my dark room out at the bright air, I felt the disparity between my internal world and the world outside. As simple as it seems, that moment has crystallized in my memory, because it was the moment I realized I had forgotten how to find pleasure in simple things. It was the moment I realized my heart had become sick.

That realization spurred me into pursuit of some of the principles in this book. Without realizing it, I had slipped into a deep disappointment—with myself, with God, with life. I knew where that would lead, and it was somewhere I didn't want to go. Of course, God met me in it and walked me through it. He showed up for me again and again until one day I realized I could hope again. I started to dream, to think about what might be possible. The unflagging optimism that had been my norm began to return. One night, while talking with Mark, I discovered that I could once again say, "With God, anything is possible," and feel the faith and hope of that statement. I believed it again.

Jesus was wearing away the numbness and cynicism in my heart and teaching me to trust him again. But it didn't happen in a moment or by accident. It happened as he patiently walked with me and invited me on the journey toward healing. As I allowed him to touch my wounded places and address the lies I was believing. As I kept getting out of bed every morning and asking for his help and facing the hard work of dealing with the ache in my heart. In my experience, the journey out of disappointment has always been a process.

Let's not pretend that Jesus' presence in our lives means that healing and breakthrough are always easy. When speaking to his disciples of the coming persecution and tribulation that would culminate in AD 70 with the destruction of Jerusalem, Jesus said, "These things I have spoken to you, so that in Me you may have peace. In the world you have tribulation, but take courage; I have overcome the world" (John 16:33). Jesus' response to suffering was not to rescue his disciples from it, but to empower them to walk in his victory through it. The same is true for us.

Whether our healing is the work of a moment or the work of a lifetime, we can know that he is with us in it, and he has overcome the world on our behalf. It doesn't always feel like we are winning when we're in the middle of the ache of disappointment, but we are. If we stay close to him, if we refuse to give up, we will get through. We will experience his peace, his courage, his victory, his hope. This is the truth about overcoming disappointment—it requires real work in tandem with the Holy Spirit, the great helper.

\*\*\*

It takes great courage to keep going when disappointment knocks at the door. It's so easy to welcome it in, to cozy up with regret and hopelessness. But we don't have to. Abraham and Sarah believed in the impossible for twenty years, and we too can keep holding onto hope, no matter what we face, because with God all things truly are possible.

Like the psalmist, we can cry out:

> Why are you in despair, O my soul? And why have you become disturbed within me? Hope in God, for I shall again praise Him for the help of His presence. O my God, my soul is in despair within me; therefore I remember You from the land of the Jordan and the

peaks of Hermon, from Mount Mizar. Deep calls to deep at the sound of Your waterfalls; all Your breakers and Your waves have rolled over me. The Lord will command His lovingkindness in the daytime; and His song will be with me in the night, a prayer to the God of my life (Psalm 42:5–8).

In every disappointment, in every loss, in every pain—God is with us, singing over us, offering us the comfort of his presence and a hope that will not disappoint.

Hope deferred turns into disappointment only if we let it. In the new covenant, Jesus has offered us a better way. He has provided for hearts healed and hopes fulfilled. Romans 5:3–5 says that even in suffering, "hope does not disappoint, because the love of God has been poured out within our hearts through the Holy Spirit who was given to us." Here we see that impregnable hope is fueled by God's love in our hearts, not by any particular circumstances. That means we can experience the tree of life even while we are waiting for desires fulfilled. We can still live in hope even in the midst of disappointment and pain.

This is the truth Jesus died to make available to us, yet many of us struggle to live in it. Often, this is because we have listened to the lies disappointment whispers to us. These lies seem like wisdom. Some of them wear very churchy clothes. But ultimately, they lead us away from the Father's heart. They block the way back to hope and take us down a darker path—the way of despair.

From my own life, and from talking with others, I've identified several key lies that disappointment uses to turn our hearts away from hope and away from God.

1. Pain is a problem and must be avoided at all costs. It's better to be numb than to be hurting.
2. After a disappointment or heartbreak, I should be able to just get over it and move on with my life.
3. When something bad happens, it must be God's will for my life. Everything that happens is part of his plan.
4. God sometimes causes bad circumstances in my life to make me a better person.
5. To find closure and regain hope, I need to understand exactly why something happened and who was to blame.
6. God owes me an explanation. If he really loves me, he will answer my questions.

In the next three chapters of this book, we will examine each of these lies and what God has to say about them. Then, in the remaining three chapters, we will look at God's solutions to these problems:

Strength in the face of pain.

Courage in the face of tragedy.

Hope in the face of mystery.

In all of it, he is with us. He is not afraid of our pain and disappointment. He weeps with us in our grief. He is all about the journey. In him, we can overcome our disappointments and find our way back to hope.

# CHAPTER 2

# The Problem of Pain

**P**AIN IS A PROBLEM. We all believe that. No one likes being in pain, because pain hurts, sometimes for a really long time. It battles against our comfort, our security, our hope. Pain is a riddle we are always trying to evade, but never quite can.

I have lived with chronic pain in my arms and wrists for the last seven years. This pain is undiagnosed by doctors. It doesn't fit any common issues. Tests come back normal. Yet, the pain persists. And it hinders my daily activities—things like cooking, cleaning, driving, typing. Writing by hand is excruciating. This is a boldface attack on my dreams. I'm a writer, not just by vocation, but in my heart. It's what God made me to do. But now, it is a calling that comes with pain. In all of this, I have discovered that physical pain has the potential to wear away at me, to diminish my strength and resolve, to sap my courage. I say *potential* because pain does not *have to* have this effect, but it often does.

In my own battle against the wearing presence of pain, I realized something important—pain is not the problem. Not really.

A few years ago, I came across a blog post written by Ann Voskamp titled, "How Real People Make (Real) Love." In it, she says pain is unavoidable in life, but we have a choice about how we respond to it. We can choose to have a hard heart or a broken heart.[1] This idea shook everything I had believed about pain. I had thought pain was the problem. I had lived with the illusion that avoiding pain would make me happy—that the pain-free life was my goal. Yet Jesus didn't run from pain. He embraced pain as a necessary part of his pursuit of us. For the joy set before him (relationship with us), Jesus said *yes* to the pain of the cross (see Heb. 12:2). Love led him into pain. If Jesus' love made him vulnerable to pain, caused him to embrace pain for our sakes, then pain couldn't be the real problem.

About the connection between love and pain, C. S. Lewis wrote in *The Four Loves:*

> There is no safe investment. To love at all is to be vulnerable. Love anything and your heart will certainly be wrung and possibly be broken. If you want to make sure of keeping it intact, you must give your heart to no one, not even to an animal. Wrap it carefully round with hobbies and little luxuries; avoid all entanglements; lock it up safe in the casket or coffin of your selfishness. But in that casket—safe, dark, motionless, airless—it will change. It will not be broken; it will become unbreakable, impenetrable, irredeemable.[2]

*To love at all is to be vulnerable.* If pain is the problem, then hardening our hearts—barricading them against the onslaught of life—seems the logical choice. Yet, a hard heart will lead to a different and deeper pain, because a hard heart becomes immune to love. I know this, because I lived it.

In my teen years, several painful events caused me to shutter my heart. I didn't know how to process the pain, rejection, and violation I had experienced. I didn't consciously chose to harden my heart, but the accumulation of unprocessed and unhealed pain created a numbness in me. Looking back, I see that I did the best I knew how to, but I lacked the tools to truly heal. For me, being OK looked like telling my heart it needed to be quiet.

Then, during my final year of college, a predatory person who had played a significant role in this pain died unexpectedly. I had purposefully avoided him for years. The news of his death shook me. I felt sad—but also relieved. I felt guilty for feeling relief. I felt angry to be in that situation, angry that a person who should have been special to me was instead a terror.

The pain of that relationship came rushing back in on me, but I had forgotten how to feel. I didn't know how to embrace the pain and let it go. It felt stuck in my gut, an ache in my chest and my throat. I needed to cry, but I hadn't in years. I didn't know how. So I called a friend and asked if she wanted to watch a movie—something really sad. It was the only way I knew to cry. If I couldn't cry for my own pain, I could cry for someone else's.

This hardness or numbness in my heart followed me for years. Once, a friend told me she felt like it was impossible to get to know the real me. She felt like I always had a wall up, like everything I said was too measured, was not genuine. That hurt me, of course. I didn't understand what she meant. I was trying to be real. I didn't realize I'd shut my heart down. I didn't realize that being able to tough out the hard moments came with a price—my ability to connect in wholehearted love.

My journey into wholeheartedness took time. Meeting my husband, Mark, made me aware of my emotional lack. I kept bumping up against walls in my heart, and now I had a compelling reason to find a way through. It wasn't easy. I had spent so many years terrified of really feeling, of risking whole-hearted love. Mark was patient with me, but I was still quick to push my feelings down, to tell my heart to be quiet. Mark spent the first few years of our marriage asking me what I really wanted—but I didn't know. I couldn't tap into the real me, because my heart was numb.

During the second year of our marriage, I had an encounter with another predatory man—this time someone who had been a mentor to Mark from a distance. We were finally meeting in person—but it didn't go how I imagined. Mark and I both felt betrayed and disappointed. I found myself bumping up against some of the same frustrations I felt the night that other man died. I knew I should feel things, that deep down my heart did feel things, but I couldn't connect to it. My heart was still numb, but this was my tipping point.

I called one of my sisters and asked her how she processed these sorts of things. I knew I couldn't let it go unless I felt it, but my heart was shut. She told me she had realized, in her own journey, that she had also shut down her emotions and told them to be silent. A wise friend had counseled her to apologize to her emotions for telling them to be silent, for taking away their voice. "I know it sounds weird," she said, "but it has helped." She had repented to that part of her soul—which was never meant to be silenced—and invited her emotions to be heard, but in submission to the Spirit of God.

I did think it was weird, but I also really wanted to be free. After I got off of the phone, while sitting on the edge of my bed, I asked God to help me set my emotions free. I apologized to them for silencing them. I asked them to speak again. I told them their voice mattered, even if what they said wasn't always comfortable or rooted in the truth. I said I wanted to feel my emotions, but that they needed to stay submitted to God's truth and the Holy Spirit's leadership in my life. Nothing remarkable happened outwardly that day—but everything changed. The numbness began to fade; my emotions found their voice. The heart of stone became a heart of flesh.

I had finally stepped into God's great promise—the new covenant heart fully alive: "I will give you a new heart and put a new spirit within you; and I will remove the heart of stone from your flesh and give you a heart of flesh" (Ezek. 36:26). Since that moment in my early twenties, when pain has walked into my life, my instinctive prayer has been, "Papa, please keep my heart tender."

I know now, no matter what the cost, I cannot go back to the hard-hearted life. If I want to live—truly live—I need to say *yes* to the pain.

We find a metaphor for this in the disease known as leprosy. In Bible times, people feared leprosy, a contagious bacterial disease that attacks the nervous system, causes nerve damage, and eventually can lead to crippling of the hands and feet, paralysis, and blindness. Nerve damage inhibits feeling and the body's normal pain signals. Because of this, people with leprosy often don't realize the harm they are causing themselves. If my foot is broken, but I can't feel the pain, I'll keep walking on it, making it worse until the damage is irreparable and the limb is lost.

When we think of pain in the body, we know it serves a vital purpose. Pain warns us that something is wrong. Pain is meant to keep us safe, to help us heal. So, pain is not the problem; the wound that sets off the alarm of pain is the problem. If we can't hear the alarm, we are in trouble. Just ask a leper.

A hard heart is very much like leprosy. It numbs the pain, but it doesn't remove the hurt. Instead, it allows that hurt to remain, to spread and grow until parts of our lives are falling to pieces, and we have no idea why. As far as we know, Jesus healed every leper he met. The unfeeling life is no way to live.

A hard heart is its own kind of pain.

\*\*\*

During my college years, a close friend's father died, and I attended his funeral. At the graveside service, my friend, her mother, and her brother sat on chairs facing the casket. It was a cold, but crisply beautiful day. The sky felt so large and blue above us as we gathered to say goodbye. Near the end of the service, my friend and her mother began loudly wailing. Everything was silent, listening to their pain, making space for it as it roared out of them.

I will never forget that day, because up until that time, I had never seen or heard someone's unrestrained grief. I came from a world of stoicism, where funerals were quiet and somber. We might cry a few silent tears—but roar with grief? Never.

Their grief—so loud and open—shook me. It scared me, yet I also longed to be so free. *What if I could wail my pain? What if I could let it out?* It seemed impossible. I did not believe I could be loved in that place. My heart was too numb, and too afraid, no matter how much I wanted it. I could not risk letting my pain have a voice.

Not until many years later did I learn to wail. We were in the middle of the hardest season of our lives—walking through the aftershocks of trauma with our daughter. One morning, I received a distressing phone call. It wasn't the news I wanted to hear. After a year full of hard news and disappointment, it felt devastating, like someone had kicked down my final support. And when I hung up, I sat down on my daughter's bed, and the grief of that moment was so much that I felt I might die. All I could do was wail. For the first time in my life, grief audibly burst out of me. I could not hold it in. The ache in my heart finally found its voice. It was loud and raw and ugly, and I hated it. But afterward, I felt a measure of peace. I felt the nearness of Jesus.

The months that followed were unbelievably hard. But I believe that moment of unfettered grief freed and strengthened my heart. The ability to release the pain was essential to my perseverance in that season and to my eventual healing. I kept going forward, kept hoping, kept stepping into peace. That season could have broken me. It could have settled me firmly in disappointment and disillusionment. But it didn't. God took care of my heart. He kept my heart tender and taught me to feel even more deeply. It seems counterintuitive, but embracing the weakness of pain has made me stronger. I found that when I let myself feel the pain, it loses the power to break me.

Recently, I had a similar experience. Nearly fifteen years into our marriage, I uncovered a wound I'd buried in the first year of our marriage. At the time, I didn't know how to process the hurt, so I did what I'd always done. I pushed it down and ignored it. I told myself it didn't matter, and I'd be fine. For many years, it was mostly forgotten. Yet it was still there, unresolved, silently eking away at my ability to love and connect wholeheartedly. At the same time, I had an ongoing struggle in a particular area, and I could not identify its root. No matter how much I prayed about it or talked with Mark about it, I couldn't figure out how to get free of it. Years of this struggle had created a deep frustration in my heart. I longed for breakthrough—but I could not find the key that would unlock the door.

Then, one day, as I talked with God about this frustration, he brought that unresolved and forgotten wound to mind. "You never let yourself feel the pain of that experience," he told me. His words hit hard. I knew he was right. I now knew the connection between embracing the pain and finding healing.

"OK," I said. "I am ready. Let me feel the pain so that I can let it go." For nearly two days, the pain and grief of that long ago experience washed over me. It felt overwhelming and counterproductive—like I was living in the past. I felt silly that something from so long ago could still affect me so deeply. But I knew if I discounted what I felt I wouldn't be able to embrace the process of healing. We don't get to choose how things affect us or to judge whether our pain is legitimate or warranted by our circumstances. We simply get to choose whether we will face what we feel and walk through it with Jesus. With that in mind, I pushed on with one goal—to simply feel. To refuse to stifle or silence the pain. To walk through the grief with Jesus, allowing him to breathe on the pain and the disappointment it had borne in my heart.

Disappointment is, ultimately, the great danger of pain. When we refuse to face pain, to let it speak, to let it go—it births a monster of disappointment in our hearts. The hard heart fears pain above all things. It is an expert at avoidance, yet it fights a losing battle, because pain that is not felt cannot leave. It builds a home in our hearts, like a hidden parasite, making our hearts sick.

We were not made to live in long-term pain. We were made to feel the pain (our hearts' alarm system) and, with the help of God, walk through the pain into healing. What that journey through pain looks like is unique to each person. Whether we grieve loudly or quietly, inwardly or outwardly, we must refuse to silence the pain. We must allow ourselves to feel, and keep feeling, until we have found healing and resolution. This is the only way to live in wholeness. Avoidance leads to unresolved pain, which leads to disappointment and despair.

\*\*\*

Several months ago, I sat down to lunch with a friend, and I told her I felt like I was going through a mid-life crisis. In the last three years, our family had experienced significant trauma and loss on multiple fronts. Now that we were out of crisis mode, I had begun to feel like I didn't know who I was anymore or how to get back to myself. I found myself questioning dreams I'd hoped and prayed into for years. *Do I really want to do that? What do I even want to do?* These big questions scared me.

I felt like I should be able to just "get over" what had happened, to "move on" with my life. That is the usual advice. But it wasn't working. The ache in my heart wouldn't let me. I found myself wondering, *How does one get over something like that, after all? How does one "move on" when everything has changed?* I don't know the answer to that question. What I do know is: That it is the wrong question to ask.

After sharing all of this with my friend, I asked her, "Is something wrong with me?"

She smiled and told me she'd felt that way before, like she'd lost herself after a major life change. "It's because you're not the same person you were before that happened," she said. "What happened changed you."

She was right. I'd felt lost because I'd been trying to find my way back to who I used to be instead of looking forward to the new. The popular idea that we can just "get over it" implies that we can return to how we were before, that life can go on as if the hard things never happened. The truth is, trauma and loss change us forever. The way back to hope is not found in returning to who we once were, but in finding out who we will become. There is no going back to the person I was before I knew what it is to experience this kind of loss and pain.

It's like Frodo, in the *Lord of the Rings,* returning to the Shire and finding that things can never be as they were before, because the pain of his journey has irrevocably changed him:

> "Are you in pain, Frodo?" said Gandalf quietly as he rode by Frodo's side.
>
> "Well, yes I am," said Frodo. "It is my shoulder. The wound aches, and the memory of darkness is heavy on me. It was a year ago today."
>
> "Alas! There are some wounds that cannot be wholly cured," said Gandalf.
>
> "I fear it may be so with mine," said Frodo. "There is no real going back. Though I may come to the Shire, it will not seem the same; for I shall not be the same. I am wounded with knife, sting, and tooth, and a long burden. Where shall I find rest?"
>
> Gandalf did not answer.[3]

Many of us have experienced losses and disappointments that have left their mark on us. Even after we heal, the scars remain. These experiences change us forever.

Recently, I listened to a TED talk by Nora McInerny called, "We Don't 'Move On' from Grief. We Move Forward with It."[4] In it, she tells the story of losing a baby, losing her father, and losing her husband to cancer—all within the space of two months. She explains that she found healing through being present in the pain and embracing the ways these loved ones—and the experience of losing them—had changed her and made her who she is now.

What she said resonated deeply with me. And it freed me. The truth was, I didn't need to "get over it." I didn't need to act as though the pain had never happened. When Jesus came to see the sisters Mary and Martha after their brother had died, he didn't tell them to "move on." He wept with them. Even though he knew the solution to their pain, and he was about to unleash it, he stopped to grieve with them first. Then Jesus raised Lazarus from the dead. Mary and Martha got their brother back, but I know the grief of losing him—even just for three days—changed them. They didn't go back to the way things were, even though Lazarus didn't stay in the tomb. They moved forward together into something new.

Imagine sitting down for a meal, saying goodnight for the evening, walking through all the daily routines, realizing—*You were dead, and now you're alive.* There's no going back from an experience like that.

The hard heart wants us to believe we can avoid the pain, we can just move on and life will be as it was, undisturbed by grief. The truth is, the pain will never leave until we let ourselves feel it and heal from it. And that process changes us forever. Even Jesus was changed by pain. The man who died on the cross was the same man who rose from the dead three days later—and yet he was also different. When he walked through walls to show his disciples the wounds in his hands and side, we see that his brokenness made him mighty. He is the same man who taught and loved and worked wonders, but he is now also the man who sits at the right hand of the Father with fire in his eyes.

When the apostle John saw the risen Christ in his vision—called the revelation of Jesus Christ—he fell on his face like a dead man. John was Jesus' closest earthly friend, yet even he trembled at the revelation of the risen Christ. Like Christ, when we embrace the walk through pain and allow him to heal our hearts, we find ourselves transformed. I believe this transformation leads us into a life more fully alive. A life of mighty, fierce, fiery-eyed love.

God has equipped us to walk through grief and loss. And if we invite Jesus along on our journey, he will weep with us, he will offer us hope and healing, and he will enable us to change for the better. We all know people who have walked through pain and allowed it to make them bitter or angry. Grief apart from Jesus will do that to us. But when we let him lead us into the new, trusting him to steward our hearts, even the hardest moments can bear good fruit in our lives.

I'm thankful for my friend who told me I'm not crazy and that I don't need to just "move on," but instead, move forward. I'm still learning to be present in my healing journey. I no longer expect to "get over it." What I do expect is that this healing I'm walking into will not just be for me. The ways I have grown and will grow, the increased depth and nuance with which I see life and others, will make me into a better friend—a friend who loves like Jesus. He left his perfect home and embraced the path of pain in this imperfect world because that path led him toward us.

Pain is the child of an imperfect world. Pain comes from loving the people and things that cannot be perfect, that cannot stay forever. It comes from the choice to dream and desire, knowing that our dreams and desires cannot be perfect, will sometimes fail. The choice to love comes with the realization that we will eventually lose what we love (in death, if not before) and that the act of loving makes us vulnerable. Yet, we are made to love. Like Jesus, like our Father, we are lovers by nature. Our hearts cry out for connection and purpose, even though we know it will hurt.

If pain is the problem, then love and hope are the real problems. This is the thesis of a hard heart. It argues, if I don't risk my heart in love or hope, I will be safe from pain—from disappointment, rejection, betrayal, loss. But this is an impossibility. A hard heart keeps fomenting the secret pain—like a leper running on a broken foot—until one day something snaps, and we can no longer keep going.

Instead, what if love and hope in the face of pain is the answer to our fear of pain and the weight of disappointment?

Both terrifying and miraculous, this is the door Jesus opens for us—to be filled with fierce and courageous love that burns for the moment and hope that will not lose heart, no matter what may come.

This is the only way to heal from pain and find our way back to hope.

# CHAPTER 3

# The Problem of God's Will

SEVERAL YEARS AGO, WHILE Mark and our son, Evan, waited to pick up our car at the dealership, the salesperson told them the story of her pain and disappointment. She had been a teacher at a Christian preschool for many years. It was her passion, and she loved it. Then, her brother died unexpectedly, and it shook her world. Though grieving, she pushed on and continued to invest in her kids at school. Then one day, the superintendent of the school called her into her office and told her that several parents had complained that her countenance had changed, that she seemed depressed and unfit to teach their children. They fired her that day. No second chances, no sympathy for her grief, no help in healing.

That's how she ended up at the dealership—needing work and willing to do whatever she had to do to support herself, even something so far from her passions. She shared with Mark how the experience had shaken her faith. *Why had God brought such tragedy and loss into her life?* she wondered.

"God didn't do this to you," Mark said. "It's OK to blame the people responsible."

"It is?" she said, leaning forward, looking at him intently. "I thought it was wrong to blame them. I guess I blamed God instead."

"People made those hurtful choices—not God," said Mark. "He is for you, he grieves with you, and he wants to heal your heart."

When Mark and Evan left, the woman thanked them, her eyes shining with relief. She no longer had to blame God for her pain. He had not turned his back on her. He was still her savior and friend.

The details of this woman's story are unique, but her response is common. We find it easy to blame God for the tragedies we face. It makes sense. He is, after all, the most powerful being in the universe. Doesn't *being God* mean *being in control?* This is the default definition for *Godhood* that many of us hold, but it is incorrect. This understanding of God's sovereignty, which originates in Calvinism, does not align with what the Bible says about God's rulership over the world and in our lives.

The question is: Is God in control, or is God in charge? *Control* implies absolute control over every event that happens. Nothing happens apart from God's will; thus, everything that happens is his will. This is how many Christians understand God's sovereignty. It is the mainstream explanation of difficult circumstances in Christian circles: "It must have been God's will." And in this way, we attribute all kinds of horrors to God. This thinking leads to one of three results in people's hearts.

1. They embrace this belief fully, telling themselves that God orchestrated their painful circumstances to make them better people, to purify their obedience to him, or even to punish them. To accept this belief, they must repress the pain of acknowledging that a loving Father would will such pain for their lives.

2. They may try to embrace this belief at first, because that's what they've been taught. But eventually they become disappointed and disillusioned. Believing God ordained these events causes distance in their relationship with him.

3. Their belief that God ordained the painful events in their lives causes them to walk away from him. They feel hurt, abandoned, and betrayed by the Father they trusted. They conclude that God is not who they thought he was—that either he is not good or he is not powerful, but he can't be both powerful and good, considering the evil in the world. Some stop believing in God altogether.

Each of these responses is tragic. Each misses the heart of God by misrepresenting the nature of his sovereignty. Is God in control? Is he the world's most accomplished micromanager or helicopter parent who fears his children's choices? Is he the heavenly dictator who predestines every event for his own purposes? This is the picture painted by the belief that God controls all events. The logical conclusion—that every evil event of history was actually ordained and allowed by God. Such a belief turns God into a monster.

Thankfully, the Bible gives us a much better picture of God's sovereignty and authority. From the very beginning, we see God giving people genuine choices and allowing them to make mistakes. Adam and Eve didn't have to eat from the tree of the knowledge of good and evil; they chose to in disobedience to God's command (see Gen. 3). The Bible clearly indicates that choice was against God's will. To say otherwise is to suggest that God would ordain (cause) Adam and Eve to sin and then punish them and their offspring for that sin. Such a God would be neither loving nor just.

This pattern of interactions—in which God warns people against a particular choice and then they do it anyway—is repeated throughout biblical history. Unless we want to argue that God has persistently set people up to disobey his commands, we must acknowledge that people have the ability to choose something outside of God's will. This is most evident in the fact that many people die apart from Christ. We know that it is God's will that all people would be saved and come to the knowledge of him (see 1 Tim. 2:3–4; 2 Pet. 3:9), yet many do not. Even in just this one aspect of life, on a daily basis, the will of God does not happen perfectly.

God's sovereignty does not mean that he ordains everything that happens. Tragedy is not the will of God. In fact, the Bible says the opposite. Jesus said, "The thief [devil] comes only to steal and kill and destroy; I came that they may have life, and have it abundantly" (John 10:10). God's will is to bless and heal and deliver, to give us abundant life. It is the devil who brings pain and destruction into our lives. The apostle James also made it clear that God does not tempt us to sin:

> Let no one say when he is tempted, "I am being tempted by God"; for God cannot be tempted by evil, and He Himself does not tempt anyone. But each one is tempted when he is carried away and enticed by his own lust [desire]. Then when lust has conceived, it gives birth to sin; and when sin is accomplished, it brings forth death (James 1:13–15).

God is not the author of evil, but of good. James continues, "Do not be deceived, my beloved brethren. Every good thing given and every perfect gift is from above, coming down from the Father of lights..." (James 1:16–17). In these passages, Jesus and James give us a simple metric by which we can determine whether something comes from God. Is it good—does it produce abundance of life within us? If so, we can know it is a work of God. And if something has the opposite effect—destruction and evil—that does not come from God.

Clearly the Bible offers us a different view of God's sovereignty. He does not control every action, but he is still God almighty. We can understand this by defining God's sovereignty as being *in charge,* not *in control.* Being in charge speaks of authority. God has absolute authority over the earth, just as a king or queen has absolute authority over his or her domain. In a sovereign monarchy, the ruler's will is law. But that does not mean the ruler's will is always obeyed. Every kingdom contains those who choose to disobey. They do so in hopes that they will not be caught, but they know that the sovereign ruler has the authority to hold them accountable for their crimes if they are caught.

In God's kingdom, all people have choices about whether they will submit to God's authority and rulership or not. Ultimately, if they do not repent of their evil choices and receive Christ's forgiveness, they will be held accountable after they die. But that promise of accountability does not mean they are not able to make wrong and even evil choices. So much of the pain in the world results from people's sinful choices (other people's and our own). Those sinful choices and the resulting pain are not God's will.

I believe the toxic "everything that happens is God's will" teaching originates in the human fear of pain and mystery. Allowing people to grapple with their pain, to truly walk through it without dismissing or repressing it, is a scary and messy prospect. We can't control that process or the outcome. We can't offer them easy, one-size answers to explain it all away. Instead, we have to trust God to walk with them and get them to the other side. Christians are not great at this. We don't like feeling out of control. We are terrified of people's process. So the idea that God controls everything and we just need to blindly accept it as what's best for us meets that need for simple answers. The problem is, it's just not true, and it doesn't work (more on this in the next chapter).

***

Instead of telling people that their pain is a result of God's will for their lives, let's tell them the truth—that God grieves with them. He never left or abandoned them, even in the darkest moments. And he is the redeemer who brings good even out of our worst moments.

In Psalm 23, David described God as a shepherd guiding him through times of blessing and abundance (green pastures and still waters), as well as times of sorrow and danger (the valley of the shadow of death). It's important to know that God goes with us even into the valley where death seems to overshadow us. In those dark places, God comforts us with his rod and staff (symbols of his guidance and protection) and enables us to declare, "I fear no evil" (Ps. 23:4)—not because evil doesn't come, but because God walks with us through it all and gives us the courage and comfort we need. Not only that, but God introduces blessing and feasting for us in the midst of our trials (prepares a table before us in the presence of our enemies). He doesn't wait until we have fully overcome; he declares a celebration, a victory feast, even as we are face-to-face with our enemies, and he anoints us to the point of overflow.

When we know that God's goodness and mercy follow us all the days of our lives, whether we are in green pastures or valleys of death, we enter into the truth of David's declaration: "I will dwell in the house of the Lord forever" (Ps. 23:6). This house is not the promise of heaven, and it is not a church building or temple. The house of the Lord is the believer in Christ filled with the Holy Spirit. He is always with us. He lives in us, and we live in him. When we think of God as the heavenly micro-manager, we imagine him looking down upon us and orchestrating events like we are pawns on his chessboard. But God is not removed from our pain. He is our house, and we are his. He is in the pain with us. In his presence, we find what we need to keep believing, to keep trusting, to keep hoping even in the valley of the shadow of death.

The revelation that God is always with us, in the middle of the pain with us, played a significant role in my healing journey. In an inner healing session, my counselor invited me to ask Jesus to show me where he was during a particular painful event in my past. This was a revolutionary idea to me. I'd always felt alone in that memory, but the truth is, Jesus was there. I asked him to enter into my memory with me and to help me see him there. As I recalled the event in my mind, I began to feel his presence with me. I saw that he had been there, and in my imagination, I saw him weeping for me. That moment changed that memory for me. Instead of feeling abandoned, I felt known and comforted. I didn't have to explain myself to him. He understood, and he wept with me. That realization was the beginning of healing. The pain of that memory began to lose its power as I discovered that even in the valley of the shadow of death, God is present with me.

After the trauma our daughter experienced, she developed post-traumatic stress disorder (PTSD). Trauma is different from grief. I am not an expert, and I will not attempt an explanation of the difference here, except to say that trauma is deeply crippling and requires more than simply allowing ourselves to feel the pain. It is pain on a soul-shattering level, pain that almost cannot be tolerated. In the year following that trauma, our daughter floundered. She could not handle the pain. She could not even talk about what had happened or say the names of those involved. She began hurting herself. She shuttered the pain away, hoping it would somehow disappear, but of course it didn't. Ultimately, it led her to a place of deep depression and despair. She had turned her back on God, and she no longer wanted to live.

Words cannot adequately describe the agony of that season. The exhaustion of constant vigilance. The fear of what might happen when I wasn't looking. The terrible ache of a reality I never thought would be mine. The not knowing how—if—we would survive.

In the midst of that season, during my time with Jesus one morning, I tried to talk to him about my pain and how I was feeling. I hardly had words, but I knew he knew. He comprehended my grief; he heard the ache of my heart; he joined in my weeping. I felt his nearness, even as I stared down the possibility of my worst nightmare. I knew that even if the worst happened, he would be with me. He was strong enough to get me through, to bring me out the other side. I was in a literal valley of the shadow of death, and it felt like death's shadow was at the door. Yet as I became aware of his strength with and for me, I heard him whisper so clearly, "I am putting her on the fast track to freedom." In that moment, those words felt almost unbelievable. I couldn't see how it was possible. But it was what my heart desperately wanted.

I don't think I said anything in response. But I took his words into my heart, and I accepted them. I knew I could not listen to the voices of pain or fear or doubt. I had to hold on. I had to believe. That was what I chose, and I had to choose it every day. I did not feel it. I'm not sure I even fully believed it, in the sense of being absolutely convinced it would happen. Or maybe it's more accurate to say that I didn't know exactly what that freedom would look like, and I chose to entrust it to Jesus without trying to define it. And of course, I realized my daughter had a part to play. She needed to say *yes* to him, too. But knowing all that, I accepted his words and chose to simply say *yes* to them with no qualifications. That season was such that I hardly knew how to pray, and his promise became my one prayer. "I thank you, God, that you are putting her on the fast track to freedom." Over and over, I declared it.

And God did what he promised. Within six months of hearing his whisper, I saw our daughter radically transformed. It was noticeable and remarkable. It was miraculous. Of course, she continues on her journey of healing, but now she is able to face the pain and walk toward healing in partnership with God, her therapist, and us. Just recently, she completed her therapy related to the trauma—a milestone that, at one time, seemed utterly beyond reach. It has been only two and a half years since I heard God's whispered promise of freedom. The outworking of that promise has been astonishing, the change in her life breathtaking. She is living fully alive, fully in love.

I am so thankful for God's goodness and that he gave me the grace to believe. If I had believed God allowed (or even caused) that trauma, I would not have known how to face my own pain, let alone walk with my daughter in hers.

Incredibly, though God does not cause evil in our lives, he is able to turn evil circumstances around to the point that they almost seem like a blessing. I'll never forget the day when my daughter told me, "I told God today that it was all worth it, that I'm even thankful for what happened, in a sense, because if I hadn't gone through all of that, I don't know if I'd know him like I do or if I'd realize how deeply I need him." That is the kind of miracle God can do.

The apostle Paul explained it this way: "We know that God causes all things to work together for good to those who love God, to those who are called according to His purpose" (Rom. 8:28). In the Old Testament, Joseph pointed to this reality when he told his brothers that when they sold him into slavery, they meant to harm and destroy him, but God used their evil actions to bring goodness and blessing into Joseph's life (see Gen. 50:20). When bad things happen, we can acknowledge the people responsible, just like Joseph did. We can name their sins against us, and we can forgive them, because what they did was wrong. It was not part of God's plan.

Some people will look at such situations and use God's ability to work all things for our good to "prove" that God predestined those evil events in our lives. But this leads to some very tenuous theological conclusions. If, for example, everything that happens is God's plan, then people's hurtful actions against us would be justified by being part of God's plan. And before we know it, we are believing things completely antithetical to the nature of God as presented in the Bible.

\*\*\*

As a teen, I remember asking my dad what the purpose of prayer is if everything that happens is God's will. What's the point of praying about something if he's already decided what's going to happen? My dad wisely pointed me to the story of James and Peter in Acts 12. King Herod had arrested several of the leaders of the early church, including James, who he put to death with the sword. He then arrested Peter and planned to execute him as well. My dad pointed out to me that the biblical account makes no mention of the church praying for the release of James. Perhaps they assumed that he would be delivered supernaturally, just as the apostles had been previously freed from prison by an angel (see Acts 5:18–20). But, after his death and Peter's arrest, the church began to fervently pray (see Acts 12:5). In response to those prayers, God sent an angel to free Peter from prison, and he escaped execution.

My dad told me he did not believe it was God's will for James to die. Perhaps, he said, James was not delivered because the church did not pray. Then, when the church began to intercede, Peter was delivered. My dad's point that day was simple: Over and over, scripture shows us the role we have to play in bringing heaven to earth and being ambassadors of God's will. We all live our lives with genuine choices about whether we will partner with God's will or not. And when the bad things happen, we are on shaky ground if we blame God for evil and credit the work of the enemy to God's will.

Theologian Michael S. Heiser puts it this way:

> Evil does not flow from a first domino that God himself toppled. Rather, evil is the perversion of God's good gift of free will. It arises from the choices made by imperfect imagers, not from God's promptings or predestination. God does not need evil, but he has the power to take the evil that flows from free-will decisions—human or otherwise—and

use it to produce good and his glory through the obedience of his loyal imagers, who are his hands and feet on the ground now.

All of this means that what we choose to do is an important part of how things will turn out. What we do matters. God has decreed the ends to which all things will come. As believers, we are prompted by his Spirit to be the good means to those decreed ends.[5]

God's will for us is always for good, for life abundant. Believing this enables us to be the ones who walk through life's disappointments and losses to become difference-makers for his kingdom.

Theologians and philosophers have argued and will continue to argue over the nature of sin and sovereignty. My goal is not to delve deep into those theological arguments, but to look at the simple truth about God's nature as revealed in scripture. He is a good God, a loving Father who gave all to rescue us from our lostness in sin and to provide the abundance and freedom of life in him (now and in eternity). Anything that falls short of this is a misrepresentation of God's heart. He is the God who has good plans for our lives, who has provided everything we need, who fervently works on our behalf (see 2 Pet. 1:3; Eph. 2:10; Phil. 1:6).

When faced with things we don't understand, with realities that are not aligned to the goodness of God's will, let's cling to the truth of who God says he is. In the face of disappointment, we must believe he is not the author of brokenness or despair. He is the comforter, the helper, the one who is with us in the valley of the shadow of death. The one who knows the way back to hope.

# CHAPTER 4

# The Problem of Why

**I** **LOVE A GOOD MYSTERY** story. The more baffling the details of the crime, the more satisfactory the discovery of the truth. Such stories appeal to our human love of tidy endings and thorough explanations. We get to know exactly why something happened and who is to blame. But real life doesn't work like that. It's more often like an unsolved mystery. We don't always get the tidy endings we crave. Questions remain unanswered; justice is elusive.

When I look back over the difficult and painful seasons of my life, so much of the *why* of those events is unknown to me. Sometimes I know who was to blame, at least in part, but I can only guess at a motive. At other times, the reason behind my pain is completely nebulous.

When the pain in my arms and wrists first started, I thought maybe I had been working too hard. Or perhaps I'd developed carpal tunnel. *I just need some rest,* I figured. *I'll get prayer, I'll go to the doctor, and I'll be back to normal in no time.*

The doctor referred me to a physical therapist. After four months of three days a week of physical therapy, I'd found a little relief. I could cut vegetables and turn faucets without excruciating pain. But I still couldn't function normally. I still couldn't work on the computer, or write by hand, or clean the bathroom, or drive more than short distances without significant pain. And worst of all, no one could figure out what was wrong with me. I began to realize this might not be a quick fix. I started talking to Mark about whether I needed to permanently stop working.

I decided to try a chiropractor. He thought regular adjustments might make some difference, but I discovered the difference was not enough to be worth the drive and the money. Next, I tried myofascial massage, and that helped a little more, but still not enough. Then I went to see an orthopedic doctor who specialized in sports medicine. He ordered all kinds of tests, but everything came back normal. In the end, he told me he couldn't do anything for me. He suggested seeing a neurologist and undergoing more tests. By that time, I was emotionally exhausted, not only by the pain, but by the years-long process of looking for answers.

I decided to shut down my writing and editing business. I canceled my website and began notifying my clients. The loss was so much harder than I thought it would be. Not just financially, but emotionally. I'd built the business from nothing, and I was proud of it. I had made a difference for many authors and their readers. I had used my gifts for Jesus. Now, I felt naked, bereft, without my work. This was not how I imagined my career ending. With the pain, all of my writing dreams and aspirations now seemed impossible.

Disappointment was knocking at my door again. I felt like Jacob wrestling with God, wanting to know why.

*Why do I have this pain?*

*And why haven't you healed me?*

I'd sought prayer for my arms and wrists from many people. Some of them have seen many healing miracles. I did all I knew to do. I positioned my heart and words in faith. I believed (and still do believe) healing is always God's will. The Bible tells us Jesus "went about doing good and healing all who were oppressed..." (Acts 10:38). God not only "pardons all your iniquities," but he also "heals all your diseases" (Ps. 103:3). *All* is an absolute word. It leaves no room for exceptions. It denies the existence of people God doesn't want to heal. In his life on earth, Jesus met a lot of sick and injured people, and he did not turn a single one away. He healed them all (see Matt. 4:24; Mark 6:56; Luke 4:40). And when the apostles continued his ministry, they too healed all who came (see Acts 5:16). This is my theology of healing. And yet, I did not experience healing for the pain in my arms and wrists.

I had a choice to make. Would I demand an answer—put God on trial for my struggles? Or would I accept the unknowns and choose to trust God anyway?

\*\*\*

The truth is, I've never received an answer to a *why* that demanded an explanation.

It's likely I wouldn't be able to fully comprehend the answer to my *why* anyway, even if God did give it to me. I'm sure the answer to why bad things happen is much more complicated than we often realize. Consider the unknowns in any one situation—the will of the individuals involved, their subconscious issues and motivations, natural forces (weather, illness, injury, genetic factors, chance events, accidents), and the spiritual dynamics (angelic activity, demonic activity, human prayers). Most of this we will never know unless God chooses to reveal it to us.

Instead of demanding answers, I have decided to embrace mystery—embrace the fact that we don't always know why things happen, but those circumstances don't change who God is. And they don't have to change my belief in him and his promises. Healing is always God's will. The fact that I haven't yet experienced healing does *not* mean he is withholding it from me.

Some teachers like to make a formula out of healing (and lots of other parts of life). They say if a person hasn't been healed it's for this reason or that reason. The truth is, none of us knows why not everyone is instantly healed. God didn't answer that question in the Bible. Instead, he told us that he wants to heal us all. In my continued quest for healing, that's where my focus must be. Instead of demanding answers, I choose to trust that God is good and that he is my healer even before I experience healing.

When it comes to the painful and mysterious parts of life, the question *why* hasn't borne any good fruit in me. It has only stirred up anxiety and accusation. It has stunted my healing process too, because it kept me focused on distributing blame rather than finding healing. It is OK to not know why something happened—to recognize that God did not ordain those events—but not need to have an opinion on or explanation for why they happened. It's OK to say, "I don't know why that happened." God doesn't need our defense; he just needs our trust.

Mystery is part of life as a human. When we refuse to accept mystery, we put ourselves on the road to bad theology. It's foolish to try to explain what God hasn't explained. Life doesn't fit into a formula. Simple explanations for complicated matters (like pain and why bad things happen) always end up misrepresenting the heart of God. But even when we cannot understand the *why,* we can still hold to the truth in faith. God loves us. He is fighting for us. When hard things happen, he is in it with us. He never leaves us. This is what faith looks like, and it is how we say *no* to disappointment.

The inability to accept mystery and relinquish our need to know *why* leads to disappointment with and offense toward God. If we need to blame someone, it is easy to blame him. "After all," we reason, "if God is all-powerful, he could have stopped this event from happening. Since he didn't, it must be his fault."

\*\*\*

We see an example of this in the life of John the Baptist.[6] When John was in prison, he heard about the miracles his cousin Jesus was performing, so he sent his disciples to Jesus, asking him, "Are You the Expected One, or shall we look for someone else?" (Matt. 11:3).

This is a very strange question coming from John, the prophet who announced the ministry of Christ by saying, "Behold, the Lamb of God who takes away the sin of the world" (John 1:29). When Jesus asked John to baptize him, John declared himself unworthy to untie Jesus' sandals, let alone baptize him (see Matt. 3:13–15; Luke 3:16). And when John did baptize Jesus, he saw the Spirit of God settle on him as a dove, and he heard God's pronouncement from heaven, "This is My beloved Son, in whom I am well-pleased" (Matt. 3:17). John clearly knew who Jesus was. From the womb, he had known who Jesus was and that his role was to make a way for Jesus' coming (see Luke 1:44; John 1:23).

In response to this surprising question, Jesus referenced a passage from Isaiah, one that every Jew of that day would have known by heart.

> Go and report to John what you hear and see: the blind receive sight and the lame walk, the lepers are cleansed and the deaf hear, the dead are raised up, and the poor have the gospel preached to them. And blessed is he who does not take offense at Me (Matthew 11:4–6).

In his words to John, Jesus alluded to a prophecy about the Messiah found in Isaiah 61:1–2. At the beginning of his public ministry, Jesus read this same passage from Isaiah in the synagogue in Nazareth:

> And the book of the prophet Isaiah was handed to Him. And He opened the book and found the place

where it was written, "The Spirit of the Lord is upon Me, because He anointed Me to preach the gospel to the poor. He has sent Me to proclaim release to the captives, and recovery of sight to the blind, to set free those who are oppressed, to proclaim the favorable year of the Lord." And He closed the book, gave it back to the attendant and sat down; and the eyes of all in the synagogue were fixed on Him. And He began to say to them, "Today this Scripture has been fulfilled in your hearing" (Luke 4:17–21).

By referring to this passage in Isaiah, Jesus was reminding John of what he already knew—that Jesus was the Messiah, and these works were evidence of his calling. However, in Jesus' message to John, he left out one element of Isaiah's original passage—release of the captives. Jesus, the Messiah, John's own cousin, is the one who sets captives free, yet John was still in prison.

Perhaps this is why Jesus ended his message to John with the cryptic statement, "Blessed is he who does not take offense at Me." Perhaps John had allowed disappointment about his circumstances to creep in, causing him to feel so offended at Jesus that he began to doubt if he was truly the Messiah. Or perhaps John's question was meant as a passive-aggressive jab—"If you're really the Messiah, do what you promised, and break me out of prison."

Regardless, it seems clear John had allowed offense and doubt to enter his heart to the point that he questioned Jesus' identity despite all the miraculous revelation he'd received. He couldn't wrap his mind around the *why* of his circumstances in light of Jesus' declaration about himself, and this unresolved *why* caused him to question Jesus' identity. This is the problem with *why*. It prompts us to demand an answer instead of trusting God in the middle of the mystery.

Our ability to accept mystery and overcome offense about the *whys* of life is an essential part of our relationship with God. The opportunity for offense tests our commitment to the relationship. Do we still trust him in the middle of the unknowns? Will we unflinchingly hold to the truth of who he says he is even when our circumstances seem to contradict him? At the core, this is what faith is all about—believing when we don't yet see (see Heb. 11).

The apostle James argued that our faith is proven by how we live (see James 2:14–26). If we truly believe, the way we live will align with that belief (not perfectly, not instantly, but progressively and consistently). One of the greatest opportunities we have for proving our faith is in our response to the unsolved mysteries of life. This kind of faith is foolish to the world, to our intellectual standards, but it is faith that pleases God.

Whether we like it or not, building a faith that overcomes offense is part of the Christian journey. When the Syrophoenician (or Canaanite) woman petitioned Jesus for help, she could have easily been offended by his response. Her daughter needed deliverance, and she knew Jesus could do it, but he ignored her. When she persisted, shouting at his disciples, he told her to go away, saying, "I was sent only to the lost sheep of the house of Israel" (Matt. 15:24). Then she bowed down before him, begging for his help, but he still refused, saying, "It is not good to take the children's bread and throw it to the dogs" (Matt. 15:26; Mark 7:27).

Most of us would take great offense at this comparison, let alone his initial refusal to listen to her pleas, but her faith was unwavering. She countered, "Yes, Lord; but even the dogs feed on the crumbs which fall from their masters' table" (Matt. 15:27; see also Mark 7:28).

Jesus then told her, "O woman, your faith is great; it shall be done for you as you wish" (Matt. 15:28). In Mark's rendition of the story, Jesus clarified that it was because of her answer to him that the demon left her daughter (see Mark 7:29). In other words, her persistence in faith, despite offending circumstances, unlocked her miracle. I don't pretend to have a perfect explanation for why Jesus acted the way he did in this story. Other than Jesus' statement about being called to the Jews first, he does not explain the *why* of his response.

Certainly, we know that Jesus' mission involved reaching the Jews first. The Jews were the people of the promise; as theologian N. T. Wright says, "If God's new life was to come to the world, it would come through Israel."[7] This was his plan. Yet many of them had wandered, had forgotten, and they needed a reminder. That was part of Jesus' purpose—as herald of the appearance of the kingdom the Jews had long awaited. Over and over he declared, "The kingdom of heaven is here!" God had chosen the Jews to be the emissaries of his new covenant kingdom for the whole world, and because of that, Jesus focused his earthly ministry on the Jews, to the exclusion of others.

Does this make him capricious or uncaring?[8] That's not how I see it. God is God, and he can do what he wants. He does not owe us an explanation. Yet even in his godhood, he bent low toward us to lift us up. He came to die, and he didn't have to. And in the case of the Syrophoenician woman, Jesus allowed the future of the-kingdom-for-all to break into his present mission to the Jews in response to her remarkable faith. N. T. Wright describes it this way:

> The woman's faith broke through the waiting period, the time in which Jesus would come to Jerusalem as Israel's Messiah, be killed and raised again, and then send his followers out into all the world (28.19). The disciples, and perhaps Jesus himself, are not yet ready for Calvary. This foreign woman is already insisting upon Easter.[9]

What stands out to me is the importance of our perspective. We can get hung up on what feels like exclusivity in Jesus' plan and allow offense to enter our hearts. Or we can find his heart in the way he altered the plan, the way he moved up the timetable for this woman when he didn't have to. We may never understand the *whys* of life, but we can see God's love for us. And we can embrace faith in the middle of the unknowns because of his love. When we do, we begin to step into the depth of faith that releases his kingdom into the most unlikely places.

In her book, *A Circle of Quiet,* Madeline L'Engle tells the story of how all her intellectual doubts about God and the salvation story were resolved through an act of love. Something terrible had happened, and Madeline felt helpless to alleviate the pain of the two friends who were involved. Then, a spiritual leader she knew stepped in and did something to help her friends in a way that deeply impacted her heart. She writes:

> This was the moment of light for me, because it was
> an act of love, Love made visible. And that did it....
> Because of this love, this particular (never general)
> Christian love, my intellectual reservations no longer
> made the least difference. I had seen love in action,
> and that was all the proof I needed.[10]

Faith based on intellectual understanding or anything
other than God's love for us will ultimately fail us, because
faith requires mystery. It cannot be faith if we fully understand (see Heb. 11:1).

\*\*\*

When God rescued the Israelites from Egypt, he led
them toward Mount Sinai on their way to the promised
land. Just three months after they had left Egypt, they
arrived at Mount Sinai, and Moses went up the mountain
to meet with God. God gave him this message for the people of Israel:

> You yourselves have seen what I did to the Egyptians,
> and how I bore you on eagles' wings, and brought
> you to Myself. Now then, if you will indeed obey
> My voice and keep My covenant, then you shall be
> My own possession among all the peoples, for all the
> earth is Mine; and you shall be to Me a kingdom of
> priests and a holy nation (Exodus 19:4–6).

Here God revealed his plan for Israel—that they would
become his own people who would be a kingdom of

priests. A kingdom of priests is a kingdom in which every person knows and relates to God personally instead of via a select group of priests or mediators. That is what we have in the new covenant (see Rev. 1:6; 5:10), and it seems that was God's desire for Israel when he set out to make a covenant with them. Initially the people liked the idea, and they responded, "All that the Lord has spoken we will do!" (Exod. 19:8).

Yet, when the time came, something went wrong. The Mosaic covenant (or old covenant) was not a covenant with a kingdom of priests. It was a covenant administered *by* priests, and the mass of the people did not know God. They only knew what the priests taught them about God. So what happened? How did God set out to give them a covenant of relationship and instead end up giving a covenant of rules?

The answer is that the people of Israel gave in to offense. When God came down on Mount Sinai, it was a terrifying sight. The Bible says he came down in fire and that the smoke was like that of a mighty furnace. Also, the entire mountain "quaked violently" (Exod. 19:18). When Moses spoke, God answered him in thunder. He had also warned the people not to stare at or touch the mountain so that they wouldn't die (see Exod. 19:12, 21–24). In the face of this demonstration of God's greatness and holiness—even though they had just experienced his great care for them as their deliverer and provider—the people were terrified.

> All the people perceived the thunder and the lightning flashes and the sound of the trumpet and the mountain smoking; and when the people saw

it, they trembled and stood at a distance. Then they said to Moses, "Speak to us yourself and we will listen; but let not God speak to us, or we will die" (Exodus 20:18–19).

Moses exhorted them not to be afraid. He told them God was simply testing them, testing their hearts and their commitment to him (see Exod. 20:20). God had set before them an opportunity for offense, hoping they would respond in trust and faith, but they did not. Their terror at the revelation of God's power caused them to forget his love and goodness toward them. They rejected the opportunity to be a kingdom of priests, to have intimate relationship with God, asking Moses to be their mediator instead.

God gave them what they asked for. He gave them priests and prophets to speak to them on his behalf. I do not believe this was what he wanted. And the arrangement did not work out well for the Israelites either.

The Israelites had pushed God away, kept him at a distance, promising to keep his laws, but not ever wanting to know his heart. This, I think, is why several times in the Old Testament we see God looking forward to a time when he would make a new covenant with people—a covenant that would touch their hearts and enable them to live righteously because of their relationship with him (see Ezek. 11:19; 18:31; 36:26; Jer. 31:33; Prov. 3:3; 7:3). He has always longed for that relationship, from the very beginning, but because of offense the Israelites misunderstood his heart and responded in fear, not faith.

In the forty years after that, while the Israelites wandered in the wilderness, God continued to test them to know what was in their hearts (see Deut. 8:2). But over and over, they responded not with faith and trust, but with fear and accusation. The writer of Hebrews reflects on this choice:

> Therefore, just as the Holy Spirit says, "Today if you hear His voice, do not harden your hearts as when they provoked Me, as in the day of trial in the wilderness, where your fathers tried Me by testing Me, and saw My works for forty years. Therefore I was angry with this generation, and said, 'They always go astray in their heart, and they did not know My ways'" (Hebrews 3:7–10).

It seems the Israelites were prone to going astray in their hearts because they did not know God's ways. Knowing God's ways implies a level of intimacy. Though they saw God's works (his actions), they misunderstood him because they did not know his ways (his heart). They did not drink deeply of his goodness and lovingkindness, and therefore, when hard things happened, they blamed God. They allowed disappointment and offense through the door, and they put God on trial, demanding answers instead of choosing to trust him. This is a lesson and warning for all of us.

The life of faith is a life that embraces mystery—even mystery that is painful. And it responds to the unknown, the unanswered, with trust.

***

The Bible is full of things that can't be explained. So are our lives.

When the trauma event happened in our daughter's life, the question of *why* hung heavily in my heart. For the first week afterward, I felt the constant need to weep, and I could hardly function. Part of our response to the trauma was the decision to immediately begin homeschooling our kids. A friend from our church helped me figure out all the necessary paperwork and curriculum—an overwhelming task in the middle of a school year, in the middle of grief. Several times during the process, I physically and emotionally broke down.

Everything in me railed against the sudden turn our lives had taken. Everything demanded some kind of explanation for an event I could not even begin to comprehend. *How could Christian adults do something like this? How could they make a choice so obviously devastating to a child? How could they possibly claim to be acting in love while doing something so spiritually and emotionally abusive?*

Every time I have shared the details of this event with another person, that person has responded in shock and disbelief. I remember telling a good friend of mine, and her shock reverberated with expletives. She then apologized for her language. I told her she didn't need to. Some things deserve the worst words.

In the months that followed, my mind continued to wrestle with the trauma, trying to find a *why* that made sense. I knew God wasn't at fault, that it wasn't his plan, but my heart and mind remained chaotic with questions. I did not want to accept an unknown. I thought that if I could understand the *why,* it would be somehow easier to accept what had happened and move forward. But at the same time, I knew that answers were improbable. It would take a miracle. Either the person to blame would need to repent, or God would need to explain it to me himself.

As I cried out, demanding an explanation from God, the chaos in my mind and heart grew louder. But when I found a way to be still, I heard him say, "It's going to be OK." At first, this frustrated me. I wanted answers and solutions. I wanted something definitive and tidy and logical. I wanted a single-solution math problem, but God was writing a beautifully nuanced story. He wanted to take me on a journey. Answers and solutions wouldn't fix the pain in my heart. Instead, what I needed was his presence with me.

Over the space of a few months, I slowly began to accept the not knowing, and I found that the more I did, the more peace I had. I could let it go and trust it to him. It really would be OK—not because I got answers or justice, but because God is present with me in the middle.

One of the greatest temptations we face is to blame God for the mysteries—for the hard times and the things we can't understand. But doing so will keep us from taking our next step with Jesus. It will sabotage the miracles we're waiting for.

The Book of James reminds us that "God is opposed to the proud, but gives grace to the humble" (James 4:6). When faced with the unknowns of life and the temptation to become disappointed and offended at God, we always have a choice between these two positions. We can choose to proudly put God on trial, demanding explanations, or we can humbly draw near to God. When we turn to God in our pain, without accusation, he will always draw near to us and comfort our hearts. "Draw near to God and He will draw near to you" (James 4:8). We see this clearly in the story of the Old Testament prophet Elijah.

Elijah fell into disappointment after his epic clash with the prophets of Baal. Even though he had just experienced a major victory, when Jezebel threatened his life, Elijah ran away into the wilderness and asked God to let him die. God sent an angel to feed and strengthen Elijah; then he told him to go to Mount Horeb. When God asked, "What are you doing here, Elijah?" (1 Kings 19:9), Elijah responded:

> I have been very zealous for the Lord, the God of hosts; for the sons of Israel have forsaken Your covenant, torn down Your altars and killed Your prophets with the sword. And I alone am left; and they seek my life, to take it away (1 Kings 19:10).

Elijah's words show the grief and disappointment in his heart. Though he didn't blame God, he had become weary of the fight. His hope had become sick.

It seems like Elijah expected the showdown with the prophets of Baal to result in an immediate, full-scale conversion of the people of Israel back to God. But that's not what happened. Even though the people had killed the prophets of Baal in response to the supernatural display of God's power, the spiritual climate of the nation had not changed (see 1 Kings 18:38–40). Even though Elijah had brought an end to a terrible famine by interceding until it began to rain, the nation had not repented (see 1 Kings 18:41–46). The problem was Jezebel.

Perhaps Elijah thought even the wicked Jezebel would repent (or die) after seeing the great display of God's power, and when she did not, but only strengthened her resolve against him, it struck a blow to Elijah's heart. He felt that all he had done had been for nothing. And if such incredible miracles couldn't cause a revival, what could? Maybe it was impossible. Maybe it would be better to just die. Elijah sank into a deep depression. He felt weary, disappointed, hopeless, and alone.

But he wasn't alone. God had preserved one hundred prophets from Jezebel's hand through the cunning of Obadiah, the man who directed Ahab's household (see 1 Kings 18:3–4, 13), and Elijah knew it. Yet Elijah felt alone and despairing because disappointment had come whispering in his ear.

In response, God told Elijah to stand on the mountain as the Lord passed by. First, a strong wind blew, breaking rocks to pieces. Then an earthquake shook the mountain, and after it a fire. Yet God was not in any of these demonstrations of might. After the fire came "a sound of gentle blowing" (1 Kings 19:12). When Elijah heard it, he knew it was God, and he covered his face and went to the entrance of the cave to speak with God.

Elijah had seen God's might. He had lived in an incredible anointing of God's power. Yet in his discouragement, the demonstration of power was not enough. Though he didn't blame God, he had become disillusioned about his calling. What he needed in that moment of disappointment was not more power, but God's comfort—the gentle whisper of his presence.

Then God asked him again, "What are you doing here, Elijah?" And Elijah answered him with exactly the same words (see 1 Kings 19:10, 14). God didn't get angry at him for this. Instead, he gave him directions for his next step. And he encouraged Elijah that hope was not gone. God had a plan for Israel—and for Jezebel, too.

He told Elijah to anoint three men—Hazael as king of Aram, Jehu as king of Israel, and Elisha as prophet in his place. Then he said:

> It shall come about, the one who escapes from the sword of Hazael, Jehu shall put to death, and the one who escapes from the sword of Jehu, Elisha shall put to death (1 Kings 19:17).

God was telling Elijah his plan for bringing justice to those who had worshiped Baal and turned Israel away from God, including Jezebel, who would eventually die at the hands of King Jehu (see 2 Kings 9:30–34).

Not only did God comfort Elijah by assuring him that he was at work, but he also provided Elijah with a friend. Elisha, who would one day take Elijah's place as prophet, became his closest companion. "He arose and followed Elijah and ministered to him" (1 Kings 19:21).

Elijah's story is beautiful to me. He was a great man, one of the greatest of the Old Testament, yet even he became weary and discouraged from the intensity of the battle. And when he did, God met him with comfort and encouragement. It is good to know that when we face discouragement, when disappointment whispers in our ears, God is waiting for us with the gentle whisper of his presence. He is waiting to give us a word of hope and to provide the support we need.

So often we miss out on this comfort and encouragement from God because our hearts take on offense against him. We blame him, in one way or another, for the things we don't understand, and this causes us to push him away. We can't hear the sound of his gentle whisper through the noise of our anger or despair.

To live in the mystery without blaming God, we must trust that faith is enough. We must trust that if God doesn't give us an explanation it means we don't need one. Jesus didn't tell John why he was in prison, but he did remind him of the revelation he already had. John already knew that Jesus was the Messiah. Elijah already knew that God was the mighty avenger. And I already know that God is a good Father.

That is the secret to my victory in the face of disappointment and mystery—my faith in who God is, my faith in his goodness. Faith says, "It's OK that I don't know why. I know God is good. I know he is with me and will get me through this. All I need is his peace."

God gives us the tools we need to be victorious in any situation. John had the revelation he needed to overcome his offense, and so do we. Paul the apostle tells us that when we face temptation, God is faithful to "provide the way of escape also, so that you will be able to endure it" (1 Cor. 10:13). God's gentle whisper is always calling us back to his heart. But disappointment is whispering too, enticing us with words of offense and accusation, pointing to the problem and causing us to question God. If we listen to its lies, it will sabotage the tools of our faith and cause us to stumble.

The question is: Whose voice will we listen to?

In the face of major loss or disappointment, the peace and hope we need to move forward are found in accepting the mysteries and trusting in God's goodness anyway.

# CHAPTER 5

# Strength in the Midst of Pain

**F**OR SEVERAL YEARS BEFORE David became King of Israel, he made his home in the city of Ziglag in the land of the Philistines. One day, he and his mighty men returned home to find the city had been burned by the Amalekites, all the livestock had been taken, and all the people had been carried off as captives. Their wealth and their families were gone, and "David and the people who were with him lifted their voices and wept until there was no strength in them to weep" (1 Sam. 30:4). This was an incalculably great loss. So great, in fact, that some of David's mighty men considered turning on him:

> Moreover David was greatly distressed because the people spoke of stoning him, for all the people were embittered, each one because of his sons and his daughters. But David strengthened himself in the Lord his God (1 Samuel 30:6).

Imagine being faced with such great loss all in one day. His home and entire city destroyed, his livestock (wealth) stolen, his two wives and all his people gone, his men so grieved that they considered killing him. No wonder David felt greatly distressed. What is a wonder is that in that moment he responded by strengthening himself in God. Offense, disappointment, and despair had a lot of talking points that day. Their voices reverberated in the wailing, in the heavy silence, in the numbness. David's men gave in to the voices of bitterness and offense when they spoke of stoning David—the man they had loyally fought under for years—for the loss of their families.

Yet David made a different choice. He firmly closed the door on disappointment and offense, and he turned to God instead. In him, David found the inner peace and strength he needed to pursue the Amalekites and ultimately to avenge their losses and rescue their families and livestock (see 1 Sam. 30:18–20).

No matter the losses we face, we also have this choice— to say *no* to disappointment and to find strength in God, trusting him to lead us into victory. And if we have already given in to disappointment, like David's men, this story shows us that we too can climb out of that pit and once again put our trust in God.

\*\*\*

The Bible doesn't tell us exactly how David strengthened himself in the Lord at Ziglag, but the Psalms give us some clues. In Psalm 22, David starts out in verses 1 and 2 with feelings of abandonment. He says that he has cried out day and night to God, yet has received no response. He has no rest. And he feels like God has let him down.

This is our first clue. David is known for being a man after God's heart and having a deeply intimate relationship with God, and he did not hold back in expressing his feelings—even feelings that seemed to reflect poorly on God. Throughout the psalms, we see David saying exactly what he's thinking and feeling, even if he later acknowledges that those feelings don't completely align with truth.

To avoid offense and disappointment, we must be willing to be completely honest with God about how we feel. David, who danced naked before the Lord, was not worried about being presentable to God or praying perfect prayers, and we shouldn't be either.

I'll never forget the moment when, as a teen, I first tried this out. After an injury to my right knee in middle school gym class, I struggled with persistent pain in that knee anytime I ran. I desperately wanted to play basketball, but even though I wore knee braces, the sport was still too rigorous. Over a few years, this became a point of offense in my heart. Though I didn't fully realize it at the time, I blamed God, and this blame caused distance in our relationship. I felt hurt. I didn't understand. And I wished so badly that things had turned out differently.

One morning, I was alone in our basement family room. I thought about how David said all kinds of confrontational and shockingly honest things to God in the Psalms, yet it seemed like God was OK with it. I realized maybe I might have permission to say what I thought, too. So I did. I told God how angry I was, how I felt like he could have helped me and he hadn't. I wept, telling him how deeply tired I was of the pain and of being excluded from activities because of it. And when it was over, I felt better. Nothing had changed with my knee, but in my heart I felt at peace. I felt close to God again. I accepted what was, and I stopped blaming God for it.

The truth is, God knows how we feel, but until we are willing to tell him, what is unspoken will be a wall between us, straining the relationship, allowing offense to grow. God doesn't expect perfection; he just wants us to be honest. Telling the truth about how we feel is a necessary step toward healing, even if how we feel is illogical or not ultimately aligned with truth.

When Mark and I have a conflict in our relationship, we must both be honest about how we are feeling. As part of that process, sometimes one or both of us realizes that our emotions aren't fair. I may have felt abandoned by Mark in a situation, but that doesn't mean he was actually abandoning me. When the emotion is brought into the light, he can care for my heart in that place, and I can recognize that my heart was unfairly building a case against him. The same is true in our relationship with God.

We must tell God the truth about how we feel while being careful not to accuse him or put him on trial. The difference is as simple as saying, "I feel abandoned," instead of, "You abandoned me!" As we talked about in chapters 3 and 4, God is not the author of the bad events in our lives, but he also does not owe us an explanation for why things have happened the way they have. Whatever has happened, God is not the problem. We aren't here to blame him, but to open our hearts so he can meet us in our pain and help us heal.

***

David knew the importance of telling the truth about the state of his heart, but he didn't stop there. In Psalm 22, immediately after saying how abandoned he feels, David says: "Yet You are holy, O You who are enthroned upon the praises of Israel" (Ps. 22:3). When he felt like God had let him down, he was honest about it, but then he reminded himself of the truth—God is holy, and we are called to praise him.

Then, in the next two verses, David recalls the testimonies of his ancestors: "In You our fathers trusted; they trusted and You delivered them. To You they cried out and were delivered; in You they trusted and were not disappointed" (Ps. 22:4–5). The psalm continues in this manner—David rehearsing his troubles and then announcing his faith that God will help him.

This is our second clue. Instead of building a case against God based on how he felt, David renounced his disappointment and unbelief by declaring the truth of who God is and reminding himself of the testimonies of God's goodness. The light of God's truth will always banish the lies we believe. Declaring who he is brings eternal perspective to our experiences and emotions. Declaring what he has done stirs up our faith for what he will do in the future. Faith declarations and testimonies have the power to not only change the way we think, but to even shape the course of our future.[11] David knew this is how we shake free of discouragement. How we get back into the fight.

Of course, sometimes this process takes time and repetition. If our loss or disappointment is deep, or we have allowed offense to take root in our hearts, we may need to repeatedly declare God's goodness in the areas where we have felt disappointment. This can be terribly hard in the moment. It demands raw faith, because it seems to deny all that we feel. Yet it is critically important.

If we fail to declare our faith in God and, instead, nourish our disappointment, it will eventually lead us into despair, the land of sick hearts and dead faith. That is not God's will for us, and it's not a fun place to be. This is why we must bravely and diligently reject the lies of disappointment and unbelief. When they whisper in our ears, we must recognize them as the voice of the enemy, who longs to bring more death and destruction into our lives. The good news is, if we refuse to feed disappointment, it will eventually die.

\*\*\*

As in Psalm 22, in Psalm 27, David also declares his faith in God, no matter what comes against him. "...In spite of this I shall be confident" (Ps. 27:3). In fact, David tells us that in the midst of difficult circumstances, he goes to war by offering sacrifices with shouts of joy and by singing praises to the Lord (see Ps. 27:6).

After telling the truth about how he felt and declaring God's goodness, David took the time to physically and verbally celebrate who God is and his faithfulness. He did this about the particular areas in which he was still waiting to see God's breakthrough power in his circumstances. David prays, "Do not hide Your face from me…Do not abandon me nor forsake me…" (Ps. 27:9) and immediately follows that prayer with the declaration, "For my father and my mother have forsaken me, but the Lord will take me up" (Ps. 27:10). When David felt abandoned, he declared in worship that even when his closest human relations abandoned him, God never would.

This is our third clue. Not only do we declare our faith in God's goodness, but we do it in worship—in a song, a dance, a shout. This is what the author of Hebrews means when he talks about continually offering a sacrifice of praise to God—"the fruit of lips that give thanks to His name" (Heb. 13:15). Praise is a sacrifice when it costs us something. And when disappointment is knocking at the door, praise contradicts our emotions, our ego, our desire for justice. In those moments, it feels like praise costs everything. And that is when it is most important.

I remember one Sunday morning when one of our kids was in the hospital (and we were not allowed to be with her). I stood in church, belting out worship songs with every ounce of my strength, tears pouring down my cheeks. I didn't know what the outcome would be. I didn't know if my child would be OK. But I knew I needed to worship, to declare God's goodness and faithfulness, even in the unknowns, with everything in me. And that moment of surrender ministered deeply to my heart. In giving my all to him, even when I felt scared for the future, I found that he is all I need.

Another time, when our family was facing financial difficulty, during his usual morning time with Jesus, Mark spent some time praying about our needs. He then felt

God inviting him to dance and praise him in advance of his provision. So in the early morning, while our kids were still sleeping, Mark got up off the couch and began to dance around the living room, praising God for his faithfulness and the ways he would provide. It was not particularly rhythmic, but it was powerful. It was surrender—the sacrifice of praise.

Later that day, we received a small, unexpected financial gift. It did not solve our problems, but it reminded us that God was fighting for us. That we could trust him to come through. Praise helped change our perspective to one of faith and trust, instead of disappointment and fear. Praise strengthened our hearts for the journey.

Our praise is mighty. It changes spiritual realities, and it changes our hearts. As we praise him, our minds are renewed. We begin to think more like Jesus. We are reminded of the good he has already done in our lives, the ways he has come through in the past. And we remember the promises he has given us—the calling he has set before us. Praise reconnects our heart to the Father, and it ignites our faith. When we praise, we are echoing the worship of the throne room in heaven, and we invite heaven's realities to be real in our lives.

At the graduation ceremony for Mark's second year of ministry school, the speaker, Bill Johnson, exhorted the students with a profound one-sentence message that I will never forget: "When in doubt, worship."

***

Just as fear gives us the opportunity for courage, disappointment and doubt give us the opportunity to give a sacrifice of praise. In Psalm 27, David did this before he had achieved the victory he needed:

> I would have despaired unless I had believed that I would see the goodness of the Lord in the land of the living. Wait for the Lord; be strong and let your heart take courage; yes, wait for the Lord (Psalm 27:13–14).

David was clearly looking forward to a fulfillment of God's goodness in his life. It hadn't yet come, but he was positioned to wait. His faith was what held him back from despair. It strengthened his heart and enabled him to wait on the Lord. Faith will do the same for us.

This is our fourth clue. Telling the truth, declaring God's goodness, and praising him lead us into the peace we need to wait on him. Like the psalmist, we can declare:

> I wait for the Lord, my soul does wait, and in His word do I hope. My soul waits for the Lord more than the watchmen for the morning; indeed, more than the watchmen for the morning (Psalm 130:5–6).

Through this process, our hearts are turned from accusation and offense to faith and trust. Our hearts are literally strengthened in the Lord, and that enables us once again to hear his voice and receive his comfort. In his presence, we realize that we don't need answers to our *whys*. We find the strength to embrace the pain and the mystery without blaming God. We discover that what we truly need is his presence with us, his peace that passes understanding (see Phil. 4:7), and his strength for the journey toward healing.

Ultimately, the journey of healing from disappointment is about realizing that restitution or a solution for what happened (or didn't happen) is not as important as healing in our hearts. God is always most concerned with our inner life and the condition of our hearts. Disappointment is so dangerous because it attacks that connection and our ability to be openhearted and trusting toward God.

Justice, restitution, and solutions to problems matter, but not as much as the health of our hearts. God's kind of peace is peace in the storm, peace that doesn't need peaceful circumstances or clear understanding. When Jesus fell asleep in the storm, he was showing us the kind of life that's possible in him (see Matt. 8:23–27). And when he rebuked his disciples for being afraid in the middle of the storm, he showed us that the alternative to unshakable peace is a life of unbelief (little faith).

God is a kind Father, and he does not judge us for struggling with unbelief or fear, yet he has made a better way available to us. Peace before understanding, faith before seeing, and hope before the tree of life. These please our Father (see Heb. 11:6).

***

Some Christians have misunderstood the call to faith in the storm to mean we must just "get over" the hard stuff by faith. As I talked about in chapter 2, the idea of "getting over" the pain and tragedy we face is a fallacy. Faith does not mean denying how we feel. It does not mean repressing our grief or pretending we are OK when we are not. Instead, faith means trusting God to walk with us through the storm and choosing to believe in his goodness even when we can't see it.

In Psalm 31, David vividly describes the state of grief and distress he finds himself in. He says his "eye is wasted away from grief," as well as his soul and body (Ps. 31:9). His life is "spent with sorrow" and his years "with sighing"; his "strength has failed," and his "body has wasted away" (Ps. 31:10). Not only that, but those who oppose him have slandered him so much that he is "an object of dread" and people scheme against him to take his life (Ps. 31:11–13).

Many of us can relate to these descriptions. We have at times felt like our grief might destroy us and that in our darkest moments our friends abandoned us. Yet David did not hide from his grief. No one could accuse him of suppressing his feelings. He didn't just express them to God and then decide to be "spiritual" and "get over it." Neither did he wallow in his emotions without finding a way to constructively move forward toward healing. He expressed his emotions and allowed himself to walk through them— all while fiercely maintaining his hope in God.

This is our fifth clue. Strength in the Lord doesn't come from denying our process, but through embracing it and welcoming God into it. Despite the many trials he faced, David chose again and again to praise God as his deliverer. He declared, "Blessed be the Lord, for He has made marvelous His lovingkindness to me in a besieged city" (Ps. 31:21). What a beautiful declaration. No matter what terror is pounding outside our gates, God's love is a miracle with us to heal and deliver.

This choice to strengthen ourselves in the Lord like David did—by facing our pain with God—is a learned behavior. For most of us, it is not intuitive. But I believe it is one of the ways God wants to renew our minds. In the new covenant, we are not to be conformed to the ways of the world—to the unhealthy ways of running from and coping with pain—but we are to be transformed as God renews our minds with the strength to face the process and find healing. This is how we move forward from grief, how we know the will of God—which is always good and acceptable and perfect (see Rom. 12:2).

Not long ago, God took me through a micro-version of this facing-the-pain-with-him process. It was the three-year anniversary of our last day as pastors. That morning the pain of that loss hit me especially hard. I grieved the loss of all we had invested over those years, and I grieved our current situation. It felt like we were so far from walking in what God has called us to, from the dreams in our hearts.

As all the emotions about that loss and the unknowns swirled in my heart, I texted a few friends, asking for prayer. Then, I headed out on my normal grocery store trip. As I drove, I processed aloud with God, telling him how I felt, but also reminding myself of his promises and his goodness in my life. *You want this even more than I do,* I declared. Then my phone playlist shuffled to Kristene DiMarco's song, "Take Courage," a ballad exhorting the heart to have tenacious courage in the seasons of waiting, because God will not fail us. I'd sung this song many times before, but this time, the words exactly matched the aching interplay between grief and hope in my heart. I wept, and I sang, and I hoped none of the drivers I passed were looking at me too closely.

I reached the store just as the song ended, looking like a mess but feeling relief. And as I gathered myself and prepared to go inside, I felt God whisper to my heart. *Remember that young mom you often see in the store? I want you to tell her she's doing a good job.* Just like that, my heart shifted. I remembered that what matters most is being obedient in the moment in front of me and trusting God with the outcomes of my life. The grief and the big questions were still real, but I felt God's nearness. I knew he was for me; I knew I could trust him. And I went into the store and encouraged that mom.

On the drive home, Jenn Johnson's song "In Over My Head" came on. That song has felt like my heart cry since the first time I heard it, and God reminded me that as long as I'm swimming out into the deep with him—beautifully in over my head—my heart will find what it longs for. My drive ended with the challenge of Dante Bowe's "Anything Is Possible," reminding me that no problem is too big for God. This time, my singing wasn't weeping, but shouting.

This drive to and from the store showed me that strengthening myself in God doesn't have to be complicated. If we simply show up in our pain and say *yes* to him, he will always meet us with the peace and the hope we need in that moment. In some seasons, this becomes a daily choice. Even an hourly choice. Again and again, we choose to be present, to let ourselves feel, to do it with Jesus. No matter how many times we find ourselves wrestling with the pain of disappointment or loss, if we come to God with trusting, open hearts, he will meet us. And that is what we need most of all.

When David sat in the ashes of Ziglag wondering if he would ever see his wives again, he invited God into his grief and asked him to comfort his heart. This, I believe is what enabled David to then ask for and receive God's wisdom for how to respond. He allowed himself to grieve with God instead of allowing his grief to turn him against God. It is no surprise, then, that after pouring out his grief in Psalm 31, David ends with this counsel: "Be strong and let your heart take courage, all you who hope in the Lord" (Ps. 31:24).

Strength, courage, hope. It's a lot like faith, hope, love (see 1 Cor. 13:13). The unending circle; the divine double helix. The heartbeat of God inside us, strengthening our hearts, calling us forward into his might.

***

After David strengthened himself in the Lord, he was able to hear God clearly for his next step. When David asked whether he should pursue the Amalekites, the Lord answered, "Pursue, for you will surely overtake them, and you will surely rescue all" (1 Sam. 30:8). And that is exactly what happened.

It is important to note that David got his outward breakthrough after he dealt with his inward grief. And the fact that he asked God whether he should pursue the raiders shows us that David had accepted that he might not be able to rescue or recover anything. Asking meant he was willing to hear God say he should *not* pursue and overtake.

And in his communion with God, he had come to peace with that possibility. If the worst happened, if his wives and property were forever lost, David knew he would get through it. God would comfort him and walk with him through it. And that would be enough.

Just a few weeks after my tearful worship set in the car, an almost unbelievable opportunity knocked on our door. Several dynamic, mighty-in-Jesus leaders asked us to consider partnering with them to plant a church. They wanted us to be the senior leaders. Multiple churches would get behind us, would send their people to join our launch team. They had the financial resources ready to help us start strong. We wouldn't have to raise support or work two jobs, but we would have to move about thirty minutes away. If we were willing, the process toward this church plant could begin almost immediately.

This invitation was completely unexpected, and for a few days, I hardly believed it. Our hearts leaped with excitement at the thought of getting back to the work we love. But we also remembered the heartache of before; we understood the risk. We wanted to know for sure what God was saying. Did he want us to do this? Would it be good for our family? Should we, like David, pursue, overtake, and rescue all? The fact that it was exciting—that it was a restoration of what we'd lost—didn't mean it was the right thing for this season. And as crazy as it sounds, as we prayed and processed, we felt God leading us in a different direction. After our relocation three years prior, our kids were just finally finding friends, getting established. Moving would disrupt all of that, again. And church-planting isn't a nine-to-five kind of job. It is a labor of love that can bleed into family time. God reminded us—our dreams aren't more important than the needs of our kids in this season.

Turning down a dream opportunity wasn't an easy choice, but it came with relief. And a new level of contentment. I knew it was right. And I felt so thankful for the healing journey God had taken us on. He had taught us to strengthen our hearts in him and find hope in his presence with us—instead of in any particular outcome. Allowing ourselves to grieve the loss of our previous church with Jesus ultimately enabled us to accept God's *not yet* in our lives. To trust him with our process, even when we don't know how it'll turn out.

Of course, this kind of trust is even harder (and more crucial) when it's not just a dream we might lose, but a person. In the book, *Parenting with Love and Logic,* the authors discuss how parents can respond to various scenarios with their children. I will always remember the section "Crisis Situations," which addresses the worst scenarios that no parent wants to face—drug use, kids who run away, debilitating injury, suicide, and so forth. The authors write, "To help us cope, we must always ask ourselves what the worst possible outcome of the crisis would be. Many times we find we are able to deal with that."[12]

They end the chapter with this:

> When a crisis erupts, we should take a moment, pray, breathe deeply, relax, write down all possible options and talk them over with a person we respect, think about our ability to cope with the worst possible outcome, and keep the faith. After all, faith is our best weapon.[13]

When walking with our daughter through the trauma she faced, this advice brought me great comfort. The worst possible outcome terrified me. I couldn't even imagine a pain and loss like that. Everything in me railed against that possibility. But when I read this chapter, God spoke to me. He told me I could get through even the worst-case scenario. With his help, I would make it. Her outcome didn't have to determine whether or not I would be OK.

And that was what I needed to know. I declared it to myself over and over. Even if the worst happens, I will be OK. God will get me through. Thankfully, our outcome was not the worst case. Like David, we got to pursue and overtake for healing and restoration in her heart and mind. Yet I know, and David knew, that no matter what may come—no matter how a particular situation works out in the end—God will take care of my heart and walk me through even the valley of the shadow of death. In him, I will be OK.

God's priority is always our hearts, and David took care of his. The psalms show us how.

- He told God how he felt without blaming God for what had happened.
- He reminded himself of God's goodness and testimonies of his faithfulness.
- He praised God exuberantly, especially in the area where he needed a breakthrough.
- He positioned himself to wait on God's comfort and direction.
- And he allowed himself to grieve, inviting God into his process.

These, I believe, are important keys to strengthening our hearts in God and overcoming the whispers of disappointment when we face loss in life. When we learn to strengthen our hearts in God, to believe him no matter what and trust that he will carry us through the worst, the lies of disappointment and offense cannot take hold in our hearts. We are impregnable in his love. We are unoffendable in his peace. We are tender-hearted, unafraid of the pain or the mystery, and free to believe.

And from that place, we step into a deeper kind of intimacy with God, an intimacy that has weathered the valley of the shadow of death. A love that has looked doubt and offense and disappointment in the face and still sided with belief. And in that place, we get to partner with God to turn the losses and pain into beauty.

# CHAPTER 6

# Courage in the Midst of Tragedy

ONCE DAVID HAD STRENGTHENED his heart in the Lord, he was ready to embark on the journey of healing and recovery. But the strength he found didn't resolve the issues in his heart; it just enabled him to face those issues and walk through them into healing. Strength is important, but it's not enough. Courage enables our strength to show up to the battle.

Healing from grief and disappointment is a journey we cannot rush. Every healing has its own timetable, and the process of healing is just as important as the eventual outcome. We don't get to choose how life affects us, how long our healing journey takes, or what our healing journey consists of, but we can choose to accept it and engage with it instead of living in denial about where we are and what we need.

On my own journey of healing, I have found that every new step requires new courage. When our hearts have been hurt by people or by life, we long to run away, to avoid the possibility of more hurt and disappointment. This is where the choice between the hard heart and the broken heart comes in—again and again and again. In some seasons, it is a daily choice. And no matter how many times I have made it before, it still demands courage. It still feels terrifying. I still want to run away.

Yet God is always there—inviting me to take that next step. To bravely tell my story. To choose forgiveness. To stop listening to regret and rehashing the *what ifs*. To accept what has happened and where I am now. To embrace the moment and the messiness of my process. To live in gratitude. To find healing for my heart and hope for my future.

God cares very much about our journey toward healing, and he gives us what we need to keep saying *yes* and keep taking steps. Some days, even making the choice to get out of bed feels hard, and the decision to do it is a victory. We have to stop thinking that being a Christian means we can't struggle. The Bible is full of stories of people who struggled deeply. Some of them walked away from God. And some of them leaned into God's grace and found the strength to get through. That is the Christian story.

Jesus gets down in the mess with us. He is not afraid of our pain or brokenness. He doesn't fear the process. He does not grow weary of our ups and downs. He knows us fully, and he is the most hope-filled person alive. He knows what's possible, and he's fighting with us for that possible every step of the way.

\*\*\*

During the most intense season of our daughter's healing journey, not many people knew what was going on in our lives. We shared with our pastors and a few trustworthy mentors and friends, but because this was her story to tell, we needed to honor her process by keeping most of the details of her story confidential. This was very lonely. It's hard to find support and care for a secret pain. But I had to set my feelings aside in that season. I couldn't face them while providing the support my daughter needed. Crisis mode and constant vigilance were our norm for close to six months. In crisis, you can't think about the pain. All that matters is the need of the moment. And that's where we were. God carried us through that time. Yet I knew that inside me the pain and grief were piling up, and when all this was over, they'd be waiting for me to sift through.

Then, at a youth event at our church, our daughter experienced a significant breakthrough. God was faithful, and just like he had promised me, he put her on the fast track to freedom. After this experience, she dove headfirst into her relationship with God, and she started engaging in therapy in earnest. Her therapist is trained in trauma-focused cognitive behavioral therapy (TF-CBT), which employs a three-step healing approach: learning coping skills, identifying distorted thoughts, and telling your story. This last step is a necessary form of exposure for healing PTSD because one of the symptoms of PTSD is avoidance.

Gradually, our daughter was able to begin talking about what had happened, not only with her therapist but also with us and with those she trusted. When she got baptized a few months later, she decided to publicly share some aspects of her story that had previously been confidential. This was empowering for her, and thankfully she received only supportive feedback from our church community.

It was also empowering for me. Suddenly, some of the big-picture events of the past year and a half had come into the light. I could now talk more openly about dealing with the aftershocks of the trauma. As I internally began processing my emotions, I also started sharing pieces of our story with close friends. I even briefly talked about it at a women's conference.

But it wasn't enough. I found that over and over I'd leave these conversations feeling frustrated. I needed something more. I wanted to bravely tell my story, but some of the memories were too painful. Some of the moments felt like dark secrets, impossible to speak, but aching in my soul. Something in me needed to feel heard and understood, but I didn't know how to make it happen. Telling the basics wasn't enough; trusting someone with the secrets felt terrifying. The last thing I wanted was for someone to tell me they knew how I felt or to give me advice about how to make everything better.

What could I do? The pain associated with those events needed to come into the light. About walking in the light, John the apostle wrote:

> But if we walk in the Light as He Himself is in the Light, we have fellowship with one another, and the blood of Jesus His Son cleanses us from all sin (1 John 1:7).

In this instance, I didn't have a sin to confess, but I needed to bring my hidden pain into the light. I knew that if I did, I would experience a greater level of cleansing and healing.

One day, as I wrestled with all of this, I felt God point me toward a particular person. I have known her a long time. I look up to her as a spiritual leader, and she and her husband already knew parts of the story. So I reached out and asked if I could come over to her house and talk with her, and she agreed. On the appointed day, as I drove the three minutes to her house and then walked the path to her door, every part of me felt shaky.

She met me at the door and welcomed me in. We sat—I on the couch and she on a rocking chair across from me. I told her the purpose for my visit, and then I jumped right in. I told her, in chronological order, the fullest version of the story I'd ever told to anyone outside our family, including several of the secret moments of pain that felt terrifying to share.

While I talked, she sat and listened silently, tears streaming down her face. She did not interrupt me even once. When I had finished, I stood up and thanked her. She gave me a hug, and I left. I still felt shaky as I walked back to my car—but this time from relief.

That meeting was exactly what I needed. From that moment, the longing to be understood in that part of my story was resolved. I no longer felt frustrated. I no longer felt a deficit in this area. Instead, I now felt freer to share about what had happened—but not from a place of need. The pain, of course, wasn't gone in an instant, but I had bravely told my story. I had brought the pain into the light, and Jesus' healing power was washing over me. I still look back on that afternoon as the pinnacle moment in that particular part of my healing journey. For me, telling my story changed everything.

Not long ago, I had another opportunity to bravely tell my story. God brought up a deep hurt that I'd never shared with anyone other than Mark. In fact, I'd been persistently resistant to the idea of sharing it because of the level of shame I associated with it. But God began to show me the impact that shame was having on my heart. Shame isn't his portion for me, but until I was willing to bring that experience into the light by sharing it with a trusted friend or counselor, I would be allowing shame a room in my life.

When God made this clear to me, I knew I had to do it. I couldn't allow shame to have the final word over this situation. Even though it felt terrifying, I opened up to a friend. And once again I discovered the freedom found in telling my story. Pain, grief, disappointment—they find power in secrecy and avoidance. They grow in the hidden places. Secrets are heavy burdens.

The light shatters that power and releases us from their weight.

Another form of storytelling is confrontation. In our daily lives, healthy confrontation doesn't need to be scary if we make a practice of kindly telling others how we've experienced them when they hurt us, while also keeping healthy boundaries with individuals who won't engage in kind and open-hearted confrontation.[14]

This is a practice I've tried to include in my life, especially in my closest relationships, even though by personality I do not love conflict. I would rather pretend like everything is always OK, even when it's not. This is another version of pain avoidance, and it isn't healthy. God has helped me see the importance of confrontation as storytelling. And he has pushed me to overcome my personal fears of rejection in this area.

Several years ago, I had the opportunity to take this belief to a new level by confronting someone I had worked for who had purposely harmed others and had betrayed my trust. By writing for him, I felt I had unknowingly participated in his efforts to manipulate and groom potential victims. The emotional turmoil caused by this person's actions toward me and many others was not easy for me to shake.

Then I received an invitation to participate in a confrontation with this person via Zoom that would be mediated by a leader who was supervising this person's attempts to find repentance and make restitution. The idea terrified me. I never wanted to interact with this person again. But I felt God whispering that such a truth-telling would be an important part of my journey. And because I personally knew and respected the leader who would facilitate the conversation, I felt confident that I would be safe.

So I said *yes*. And when the day came, I found I had the courage to boldly speak the truth. In fact, I felt fierce. Something happened in my heart when I stood up for myself and told my story while still protecting my heart. I was able to tell this man what I thought about what he'd done and even to say I didn't believe his repentance was sincere. (It's a long story, so you'll have to trust me on this.)

And when the Zoom call ended, I walked away from my phone and away from that person's influence in my life. The hold that hurt had on my life broke. His ability to affect my emotions ended that day. Every person's healing journey is different, but for me in that situation, the breakthrough moment came as I bravely told my story.

*\*\*\**

Telling my story has become an essential part of healing from many different disappointments and losses. And so has forgiveness.

Forgiveness can feel like a dirty word. Like a high note we can't quite hit. An impossibly perfect performance. But that's only because it has been mistaught and misapplied. I remember knowing I needed to forgive someone who had hurt and disappointed me, yet feeling like it was impossible. No matter how hard I tried to forgive, I continued to feel hurt and anger and resentment. I knew forgiveness was what I was supposed to do—and that it would be good for me—but I was failing.

Then in church one morning, one of our pastors at the time preached a sermon on forgiveness, and what he said forever changed my mindset. He shared the story of a deep betrayal his family had experienced and his own struggle to walk in forgiveness. Then he said, "I know a lot of you feel like you are a failure right now, because there's someone in your life who has hurt you, and you have tried to forgive them, but you still feel all the hurt and resentment." This got my attention, because it was exactly what I was feeling.

He continued, "Well, I'm here to tell you that forgiveness is not a feeling. It's a choice. If you have decided to forgive that person, then you have forgiven them, no matter what you feel. Forgiveness is a choice. The feelings will catch up eventually."

This was revelation to me. I had always judged the quality of my forgiveness by whether or not my feelings had changed. Instead, my pastor was telling me that I could just decide to forgive, and then continue to declare that I had forgiven, and eventually this choice would impact my heart. Since that time more than ten years ago, I've found this principle to be true—even in situations where I felt that forgiveness was impossible in my own strength.

In the Bible, Joseph is the first person to explicitly forgive someone, namely his brothers. In his story, we find some important truths about what healthy forgiveness looks like. First, in Joseph's example we see that forgiveness does not mean we cannot acknowledge the injustice we have experienced. Forgiveness doesn't mean pretending it didn't happen or it didn't hurt.

When Joseph revealed his identity to his brothers, he reminded them of exactly what they had done. Joseph told the truth of how his brother's choices had impacted him, and then he forgave them and released them from their guilt (see Gen 45:4–8). He also wept deeply on several different occasions (see Gen. 42:24; 43:30; 45:1–2, 14–15).

Though God had worked things out in Joseph's favor, he still suffered as a slave and prisoner, and he lost many years with his family. While he was in Egypt, his younger brother Benjamin was born, his mother died, and his father grew old. Joseph lost a lot because of what his brothers had done. Part of forgiving them was acknowledging and grieving those losses.

Second, forgiveness doesn't mean we don't set up healthy boundaries. Forgiveness doesn't necessarily mean restoration of trust, either. Joseph tested his brothers before he revealed his identity—not to determine whether or not he would forgive them, but to determine whether or not they were truly repentant. Could he trust them again? He knew that once they knew who he was, they would act as repentant as possible because of the position of power he had. This is why Joseph waited and tested them. He needed to know the truth.

When Reuben begged Joseph to allow him to take Benjamin's place as his slave, Joseph knew their repentance was sincere. Reuben was willing to give everything in order to save Benjamin. It was, in some senses, a reversal of how his brothers had behaved toward him, and it showed him how their hearts had changed. Only after this did Joseph reveal himself and welcome his brothers back into relationship with him.

Third, in Joseph's example we see that forgiveness isn't based on merit and is not dependent on the other person's repentance. I believe Joseph forgave his brothers long before they showed up in Egypt, long before he knew if they were repentant or if he would ever be restored to his family. He would not have been able to live such a pure life in tune with God's voice, even in the midst of suffering, if he was harboring bitterness all those years. Bitterness defiles us (see Heb. 12:15), but Joseph experienced great favor with God because he was pure-hearted.

Just like Joseph, our ability to forgive is not dependent on how the other person behaves. Often, we want a sense of validation—we want the person who hurt us to acknowledge the wrong. But many times people are unwilling to do this. Sometimes they do not care that they have hurt us. At other times, they are defensive and afraid to admit their wrong. Regardless, we do not need their repentance in order to forgive them.

When we forgive people before they repent, we are doing what God does. His forgiveness is unreasonable, and he has now made us in the image of Christ, the great forgiver. As new creations, forgiveness is now part of our DNA. It is not alien to our nature; it is intrinsically part of who we are.

I believe Joseph became the quality of person he was—someone who could handle nearly unlimited power without being corrupted—because in his greatest moments of loss and betrayal, he kept his heart tender, chose to trust God, and forgave those who had harmed him. When his brothers sold him into slavery, when Potiphar threw him into prison over false accusations, when the cupbearer forgot his promise to Joseph—at each of these crucial moments, Joseph could have become disappointed and bitter, but he did not.

We face many opportunities for unforgiveness in our lives. I have discovered that forgiveness isn't just for the people who did something to me—but also for those who weren't there for me. For those who hurt me through their inaction. Especially in times of grief and loss, it can feel like the people in our lives are not giving us the support and care we need.

W. H. Auden's poem, "Musée des Beaux Arts" speaks of the phenomenon of suffering alone, "…how it takes place / While someone else is eating or opening a window or just walking / dully along."[15] He describes a painting by Pieter Bruegel, called *The Fall of Icarus,* which shows Icarus drowning in the sea after his fall from the sky. As his legs sink below the waves, strangers go on living their ordinary lives, completing their daily tasks, oblivious to the boy drowning nearby. Often, the seasons of loss and disappointment feel exactly like that. Alone and unseen. Normal life continues around us even when we are drowning.

It is not easy to find people who will simply sit with us in our grief. Sometimes this is because grief feels uncomfortable. Our friends can't make it better. They don't know what to do, and that causes them to stay away. At other times, they have their own secret pains, and they aren't capable of emotionally supporting us in the ways we need. And sometimes they are just too busy. Whatever the reason, in seasons of grief we can find ourselves needing to forgive people for what they didn't do—for a lack of support or help in our lives.

I have felt that deeply at times. Yet, when I look back at those seasons, God has helped me to see that grief is lonely no matter how much support I have had. Grief is lonely, because no one else can understand what I am going through. Not really. They can empathize, of course, and they can listen and love. But ultimately the only one who can understand me in those dark seasons is God.

This realization helped me to release people from the expectations I had of them. Certainly, some people did let me down. They should have been there for me more than they were, and their absence hurt me. But others tried to be a support, and the lack I felt was simply because grief is a lonely place. Forgiving them helped me to leave the hurt behind as I walked forward into my healing. It also helped me to see ways in which I can be a better friend to others when they are suffering.

Disappointment wants us to hold on to hurt, because unforgiveness is a poison that will make our hearts sick. Forgiveness requires courage, but it also frees us to keep living with wide-awake and tender hearts. It doesn't mean we have to trust unsafe individuals or give them room in our lives. It means just the opposite—that we can be free of the emotional turmoil caused by their sin against us. We can heal, and we can walk forward unhindered by the pain and the poison of unforgiveness.

Freedom comes in forgiving others—and also in forgiving ourselves.

\*\*\*

After the trauma our daughter experienced, my initial grief response gradually morphed into plaguing feelings of regret. I found myself continually rehashing the events leading up to the trauma, overanalyzing my choices and obsessing over what I could have done differently. *If only I had done this or that. If only I hadn't trusted this person. If only I had listened to my gut.*

One of my decisions, in particular, had deeply hurt my daughter. I had thought I was making the right choice, but ultimately I was proven wrong. The choice I made ended up making things worse. The people I thought we could trust were not actually working for our good. I had failed my daughter, and I knew she blamed me for my choice.

I wished I could go back and do it over. I needed to forgive myself, but it felt impossible. The regret was crippling.

Then I read a young adult novel in which the main character experiences something that in many ways paralleled what my daughter went through. And in his moment of vulnerability, a father figure stepped in and defended and protected him brilliantly, turning a potential trauma into a daring escape. He did everything for this boy that I wished I could have done for my daughter—but hadn't, not because of a lack of desire, but because I lacked the wisdom and knowhow in the moment. Those chapters in that novel illuminated all my regrets. All my feelings of failure and inadequacy. And I wept.

I can't go back and rewrite our story. I can't undo the choices I made or erase the disappointments. But over time I realized I didn't have to allow regret a home in my heart. I could accept the way my story had progressed thus far, even with its imperfections and heartaches. By listening to regret, I had been unconsciously trying to reject my story. I had declared it an invalid path—a place I couldn't move forward from, a place God couldn't move upon.

This, of course, was a lie. God can move upon any path. Though what happened to my daughter was not God's will, the turn our lives had taken was not too difficult for him to navigate. This was my reality now, and I needed to accept it. Would I get stuck in regretting what had happened and the pain I couldn't change? Would I live in denial, or would I accept my journey for what it was? I found that forgiving myself and accepting my story so far was crucial to my future.

In his second letter to the church at Corinth, Paul wrote, "For the sorrow that is according to the will of God produces a repentance without regret, leading to salvation, but the sorrow of the world produces death" (2 Cor. 7:10). In other words, I could feel sorrow over how things had worked out without becoming trapped in regret. I could grieve and let go, knowing that God was at work in me still. He saves us out of our greatest failures and heartaches. No disappointment or loss disqualifies us from his ability to turn pain into beauty.

I imagine this is why Paul also talked about forgetting his past. Paul had plenty of choices to regret from his life before Christ—and probably from his life in Christ, too. Yet he knew that allowing regret a voice in his life would prevent him from pursuing his destiny. His strategy for success was simple. Keep looking forward. Keep running forward.

> Brethren, I do not regard myself as having laid hold of it yet; but one thing I do: forgetting what lies behind and reaching forward to what lies ahead, I press on toward the goal for the prize of the upward call of God in Christ Jesus (Philippians 3:13–14).

Courageously accepting what has happened and where I am now enables me to learn from my mistakes, to grow in the midst of my heartache, and to keep my eyes on the upward call of God.

It's easy to think our journey should make sense, that we should learn every lesson the first time, that our lives should be on a straight trajectory upward. The truth is, often our journey is messy. And that is OK.

I have a card with several declarations displayed in my bathroom. The card came with a necklace Mark bought for me from a company called The Crowning Jewels. The first two declarations challenged the way I had always thought about my journey: "My process is beautiful. I love myself exactly as I am." I have read these words over myself at least once every day for the last few years, and it has helped me to embrace my process, even when it is messy and feels chaotic. It is the journey I am on, and God is with me in it.

The Christian life is all about the process. If it wasn't, God would have made us perfectly mature at the moment of salvation. He didn't. Instead, he invited us on a courageous journey of growing in him, come what may. A journey of the moment, day after day, that is not about arriving at perfection, but about living in his embrace.

***

Saying *no* to regret and accepting our process enables us to live in gratitude—not because everything is perfect but because he is with us on the journey.

The Bible has a lot to say about gratitude. The psalms are filled with exhortations to give thanks to the Lord. And in the new covenant, we are told, "Rejoice always; pray without ceasing; in everything give thanks; for this is God's will for you in Christ Jesus" (1 Thess. 5:16–18). Thanksgiving is the culture of heaven (see Rev. 4:9; 7:12), and it is one of the ways that we step into the reality of our new creation life in Christ even while living in an imperfect and pain-filled world. Unflinching gratitude is one of the bravest stances we can take.

It is not hard to be ungrateful. We can always think of something we lack. But the Bible highlights again and again the importance of a grateful heart. The level of our gratitude directly determines the way we relate to God. The opposite of a heart of gratitude toward God is a darkened heart characterized by futile and foolish thinking (see Rom. 1:21). It is a heart that sets itself in opposition to God.

Gratitude ushers the peace of God into our hearts (see Phil. 4:6–7; Col. 3:15–16), and his peace guards our hearts and minds. Without gratitude, our hearts and minds are susceptible to offense toward God. We step into a position of accusation, putting God on trial and demanding answers or our version of justice. With gratitude, we get the peace that surpasses understanding—the peace that doesn't need to understand. And that peace keeps our hearts and minds properly positioned toward God.

The New Testament church was a church under persecution. Many of the original readers of Paul's letters were living in seasons of trauma, grief, loss, and disappointment. They faced extreme pressures and losses that most of us can hardly imagine. Yet over and over, Paul told them to be thankful (see Eph. 5:4; Col. 3:17; 4:2; 1 Cor. 15:57; 2 Cor. 2:14).

Gratitude, like forgiveness, isn't about our circumstances, but the state of our hearts. And it takes great courage. Gratitude sees life through the lens of blessing. When Jesus healed the ten lepers in Luke 17:11–19, only one of the ten lepers returned to thank Him. Too often, we live like the nine lepers, quickly forgetting to be thankful for God's blessing in our lives. Too often, our focus stays on what we don't yet have, instead of on all we have already received.

Ever since our kids were old enough to talk, we have incorporated "the thankful game" into our bedtime routine. In this game, we each go around and say one thing we are thankful for. At times, one of the kids has had a hard day or doesn't feel like playing along. "I'm not thankful for anything," he or she says.

"There's always something to be thankful for! What about your comfy bed?" I say. "Or the food you ate? Or our house, your toys, our family...." And I keep listing the everyday blessings until the child picks one to be thankful for.

Now that our kids are getting older, we rarely need to help them find gratitude, and if we happen to be rushed at bedtime and forget the game, invariably one of them reminds us, "What about the thankful game?"

One of the greatest blessings we can find in this life is the courage to be thankful—to see life through the lens of God's goodness, even when walking through pain and disappointment. And this gratitude enables us to sense his presence with us, to feel his comfort, and to embrace the journey toward healing.

Embracing this journey out of disappointment and toward hope is a choice that always takes courage. Every time we tell our story, choose to forgive, let go of regret and *what if*, accept our journey for what it is, and embrace gratitude—we take a brave and important step forward. A step toward healing in our hearts and hope for our future.

# CHAPTER 7

# Hope in the Midst of Mystery

ONE OF EMILY DICKINSON'S most famous poems begins:

> "Hope" is the thing with feathers—
> That perches in the soul—
> And sings the tune without the words—
> And never stops—at all—[16]

This bird's sweetest tune, she says, keeps people warm, even in the strongest gale, the chillest land, the strangest sea. Truly, that is what hope does in our hearts. It is what keeps us fully alive. But what happens when we meet "...the storm— / That could abash the little Bird"?[17] What happens when the storms of disappointment silence hope's song?

One of the greatest dangers of unresolved disappointment in our hearts is the crippling effect it has on our ability to hope. Faith and hope are foundations of our lives in Christ (see 1 Cor. 13:13), but when disappointment enters our hearts, if we do not deal with it, it causes sickness in our hearts.

This sickness, in my experience, primarily takes the form of disillusionment and unbelief. These take the place of faith and hope in our hearts, building a case against what the Bible tells us to be true of God. And when another difficult situation arises or when God speaks to us and asks us to take a step of faith—this sickness in our hearts causes us to respond to God with doubt or fear.

We see this in the contrast between Zacharias and Mary in Luke 1.[18] Both received an angelic visitation from Gabriel. Both heard a prophecy about a miraculous birth. Both asked how such a thing could be possible. Yet, the difference in how Gabriel responded to them shows us a difference in their hearts.

In response to Gabriel's declaration that their prayers for a child were being answered, Zacharias asked, "How will I know this for certain? For I am an old man and my wife is advanced in years?" (Luke 1:18). Gabriel then rebuked him for not believing his words, saying that he would not be able to speak until Gabriel's words came true.

Though he had prayed for a child, Zacharias didn't believe it would happen even when an angel appeared before him. It is likely that the years of waiting and hoping for a child had turned Zacharias' heart sick with disappointment. Hope deferred had done its work. And even when staring an angel in the face, Zacharias was afraid to believe. Because he hadn't dealt with his disappointment, he was terrified of believing again, because belief involves the possibility of more disappointment. If you don't believe, you can't be disappointed.

Disappointment had so crippled Zacharias' heart that he couldn't believe even when the miracle was upon him. Thankfully, that didn't disqualify him from receiving his miracle. And in the end, he demonstrated his faith by naming his son John in obedience to Gabriel's word. I imagine he did a lot of internal processing during those nine months of silence.

Not long after he met with Zacharias, Gabriel appeared to Mary and told her she would become the mother of the Messiah, the Son of God. In response, she asked, "How can this be, since I am a virgin?" (Luke 1:34). On the surface, this question seems nearly the same as Zacharias' question, yet Gabriel answered her with an explanation and the exhortation, "For nothing will be impossible with God" (Luke 1:37).

From the difference in Gabriel's response, we can assume that Mary was not harboring disappointment in her heart. Her question was a genuine question about how the miracle would happen—not a cynical, accusatory question that sought to prove the impossibility of the promise. Because her heart was open and trusting toward God, she received an explanation.

And most amazing of all, Mary was able to embrace the promise even though it must have seemed incomprehensible and terrifying to her. Without objection or qualification, she accepted God's call, saying, "Behold, the bondslave of the Lord; may it be done to me according to your word" (Luke 1:38).

Throughout the Bible, we see people responding to God's call with either fear and unbelief or open-hearted faith and hope. I believe the primary issue that determines which response we have is how well we have dealt with the disappointments and losses we have faced.

When we face the pain of our grief and walk through it to resolution, we will find the courage to trust God and to hope again, even in areas of previous disappointment and loss. But if we do not resolve the grief and just shove it down, it will become a lens we see through. It will silence the song of hope, and it will resurface to help us build a case against God's word and his goodness in our lives.

\*\*\*

Years ago, Mark had the opportunity to serve a well-known Christian minister. We were very excited for the opportunity, as we had a lot of respect for this minister and his message, and we hoped it would be a great chance for Mark to learn while doing what he loves. But that's not exactly how it worked out. Mark did learn things, and he did get more experience in ministry, but the environment was very toxic. Although this minister seemed very loving and grace-filled from the stage, with his staff he carried himself like a king who expected to be served with perfection.

This was deeply disheartening to us. And it wasn't the only time we got a view of the underbelly of a church or ministry and discovered that what was preached from the stage did not align with the way people lived their lives. Such experiences can chip away at our belief and hope for the church. When we see the mess that some people have made, it is sometimes too easy to start feeling cynical and disillusioned.

As a writer and editor, I have worked with many well-known Christians leaders. Some of them have been exactly what I hoped. They treated me kindly, like an equally valuable person. One of my clients, who I have worked for off-and-on for many years, always pays me more than I bill him for. He has a core value of generosity, and he lives it out toward me even though I am not famous or influential. Unfortunately, some other clients have been exactly the opposite. They have been rude and demanding. They have treated me like I am not important, like my worth is found only in what I can do for them.

Sadly, many people have had experiences like this. They've encountered not only the immature, but also the wolves in sheep's clothes (see Matt. 7:15). They've been part of toxic churches, maybe even experienced abuse. Church hurt is a real form of disappointment that most of us have faced at least once.

Spiritual abuse played a role in our daughter's story, and part of her healing journey has been not just returning to Jesus, but also returning to the church. It is a scary journey. The church is full of imperfect people. Some of them are still really messy. Some of them don't yet love others well. Some of them might even be wolves.

One of the reasons we chose the church we started attending after we stepped down from pastoring is the history we have with the pastors. After what we'd been through, we all needed a safe place to heal, and we knew we could trust these leaders—not to be perfect, but to genuinely love us. Our daughter had experienced deep wounds from a male spiritual leader. We needed to be in a church where the male leaders were truly safe.

Looking back, I am so thankful for the choice we made. Though at the time we started attending, our daughter had turned her back on God because of the trauma, it was at this church that she decided to give Jesus another try.

There, one of the male pastors fasted for her breakthrough for three days prior to a meeting he had with her and Mark. A meeting that ended up being a significant turning point for her. There, another male pastor stepped in when he saw her approached by an older man in a way that made her feel uncomfortable. This pastor could tell the encounter bothered her, and he took the time to check in with her and make sure she was OK. And another time, when one of the male pastors said something that unintentionally hurt her, she found the courage to tell him, and he sincerely apologized.

Recently, our daughter felt nudged by God to give a male youth leader a prophetic word during a church service. Afterward, she found herself feeling very insecure and having irrational thoughts that he probably thought she was ridiculous. As we processed it later, I asked her, "Do you think it could be because he's a male leader? That this is part of your healing journey, taking a risk and being obedient to God in relationship with a male leader?"

As she thought about it, she realized that was exactly why she had felt so insecure. When she shared this with her mentor, who is also a youth leader, her mentor told her that the word she had given this leader was very accurate to what he was going through. Our daughter didn't know it—but taking that risk in obedience to the Spirit was important for her journey and also for this leader.

Taking a risk in an area where we've experienced hurt and disappointment can feel terrifying. Yet this willingness to risk is crucial to our healing. I'm not saying we blindly trust those who have hurt us or keep returning to abusive situations. But healing from disappointment involves stepping out of our self-protective shell and risking love and hope and faith again in the areas where we've experienced disappointment.

When we allow God to guide us in these risks, he leads us into situations that have the power to release healing to wounded places in our hearts. If our daughter had never gone to church again, had never risked interacting with male leaders again, she would not have had the healing experiences she has had. That doesn't mean she has not been hurt or will never be hurt by men again. What it does mean is that her risks have given her new baseline experiences. Now, it is not just the trauma that informs her lens. Now, she has seen male leaders be Jesus to her.

These risks also serve another important purpose. They prove our own healing to us. We get to see our own courage. Recently, I've had several moments in which I was able to step back and see myself responding differently—more confidently, more boldly—and I knew it was the outworking of the process I'd walked through with Jesus and the healing he was creating in my heart. Seeing the fruit of the hard work of that healing journey is exhilarating. Risk shows me my growth, shows me I am mighty.

And when we take a risk and get disappointed again (because sometimes we will), we get to put our healing into practice. We get to say, "OK, I've faced this before, and I got through. I know I can do it again. I know I can hold on to hope." We get to practice the brokenhearted kind of love that doesn't cling to self-protection but can give of itself as Jesus did.

***

Really, this whole journey of overcoming disappointment is about learning to be OK with the brokenhearted life—learning to accept it and knowing we are strong enough in Jesus. He gives us the strength to be simultaneously brokenhearted and wholehearted. To love and hope and believe fully even in the middle of the losses and the unknowns. It is a mystery. But it is the only way to truly live.

The alternative is to let disappointment come in and make itself at home in our hearts, hardening our hearts against God, against others, against life. It will turn our hearts sick with hurt and cynicism, and it will poison our response to God and our ability to believe.

Eventually, we will become like the man at the Pool of Bethesda (see John 5:1–16). This man was crippled in his body, but he was also crippled in his heart. He had given in to disappointment. After thirty-eight years of waiting for his healing, he had no faith left. Instead of risking faith that he would yet be healed, he was content to shift the blame onto others. When Jesus asked him if he wanted to get well, he did not even say *yes*. He just gave an excuse. Jesus healed him anyway.

Afterward, the man went out of his way to tell the Jewish religious leaders that Jesus was the one who had healed him. He knew they were actively trying to build a case against Jesus. They accused him of breaking the law by healing people on the Sabbath. Instead of responding in gratitude for his miracle, this man contributed to the religious institution's blood-thirsty agenda. This man partnered in the persecution of Jesus *even though* Jesus had healed him. His heart had been so embittered by disappointment and hope deferred that even when he received his healing, his heart remained hard. So hard that he could persecute the very person who had healed him.

The hard heart is comfortable with ideals, but less comfortable with real-life experiences, because they always present the possibility of being hurt and disappointed again. The ideals of a disappointed heart serve as a buffer against further pain—but they also numb the heart to the possibility of the dream fulfilled.

In Edith Wharton's novel *The Age of Innocence,* Newland Archer becomes captivated with the unconventional Countess Ellen Olenska. However, their situations prevent them from being together. Though their interactions are brief, for the rest of his life Newland keeps his memories of the Countess in his heart as an ideal. Many years later, when all that kept them apart is gone, he has an opportunity to see her again, to renew their acquaintance and see whether something more might now be possible. Yet, when his carriage arrives at her home, he decides not to see her after all.

She had become such an ideal, an image of perfection in his heart, that he could not risk an actual relationship with her. Knowing her would mean experiencing her imperfections. His marriage had been a disaster. Who's to say another relationship wouldn't have the same outcome? Ultimately, he chose the safety of loving an ideal over the turbulence—and beauty—of loving a real person.

This story has always stood out to me as a warning about our human tendency to idealize perfection—our ideals about how a person or relationship or institution or life in general should be. Ideals, in the sense of having high standards, are good, but idealism that won't embrace the imperfections of real life and real people will prevent us from reaching for our dreams. We see this in Newland's choice not to be with Ellen, but instead to just imagine what it might have been like to be with her, because that imagination would be perfect. It could not disappoint him.

It is easy to do this, especially when we have already experienced disappointment in a particular area. Unresolved pain in our hearts caused by disappointment and loss can keep us from the process we need to heal—and the risky faith and hope we need to step into our miracle.

Disappointment wants to make everything complicated. It wants to ask accusing questions and demand answers. But faith is simple. The heart of faith is a broken heart that stays wholly alive, that keeps loving and believing. A heart that does not need to understand, but must always listen to hope's song. A heart that gives Jesus an unqualified *yes*.

The choice to risk again in faith as we walk out the process of healing from disappointment and loss will lead us into hope. As we talked about in chapter 1, the hope that does not disappoint cannot be rooted in our earthly circumstances. The whole reason we wrestle with disappointment is because our hope for the things of this life sometimes does not work out.

This is why the apostle Paul wrote to Timothy:

> Instruct those who are rich in this present world not to be conceited or to fix their hope on the uncertainty of riches, but on God, who richly supplies us with all things to enjoy (1 Timothy 6:17).

This verse clearly presents two types of hope—one that is firmly set on earthly provision and one that looks to God's provision (not just financially but in all areas of our lives). The distinction between them is slim, because it has to do with the heart. Whether we are rich or poor, healthy or sick, surrounded by family or all alone, we have the choice to place our hope in what we have or in whose we are. That is the difference between worldly and heavenly hope.

Notice that placing our hope in God does not mean accepting lack in our lives. That is not the distinction Paul was making. He made it clear that God "richly supplies us with all things to enjoy." Heavenly hope is not just for eternity with Christ, though that is our ultimate hope (see Titus 1:2). The hope of Christ also encompasses blessing and breakthrough in this life.

The question is, will we trust God to take care of us, to determine what that richness looks like, to take us on a journey of provision that is more about our hearts than our wallets? And when we experience lack or disappointment, will we trust that God is still coming through? Or will we place our hope in our own efforts, in the wealth of our bank accounts, in the strength of our minds or bodies?

Heavenly hope is rooted in heavenly realities. It sees beyond the natural to the supernatural, and it trusts in the God who is able to raise the dead things back to life. Hope declares, without wavering, "He who promised is faithful" (Heb. 10:23). It is "an anchor of the soul, a hope both sure and steadfast" (Heb. 6:19).

When describing the difficulties of his missionary journeys to the Corinthians, Paul wrote:

> For we do not want you to be unaware, brethren, of our affliction which came to us in Asia, that we were burdened excessively, beyond our strength, so that we despaired even of life; indeed, we had the sentence of death within ourselves so that we would not trust in ourselves, but in God who raises the dead; who delivered us from so great a peril of death, and will deliver us, He on whom we have set our hope. And He will yet deliver us (2 Corinthians 1:8–10).

Here we see this same dichotomy between earthy and heavenly hope. Paul and his companions suffered almost to the point of death. In the natural, they had no hope. Yet they put their hope in God as the one who raises the dead, and he delivered them.

This is the hope that will not disappoint—hope that is set on Christ. Such hope does not guarantee that everything will go perfectly for us or that we will never experience disappointment or loss. What it does guarantee is that Jesus will be with us in the storm—and he will deliver us and guide us on our journey of healing. He will not leave us in our misery. He will work priceless miracles in our hearts.

In him, we have not only the hope of his grace at work in us for righteousness and glory (see Gal. 5:5; Col. 1:27), but also his comfort and strength for us in the middle of every season (see 2 Thess. 2:16–17).

Later in that same letter, Paul also wrote, "We are afflicted in every way, but not crushed; perplexed, but not despairing; persecuted, but not forsaken; struck down, but not destroyed" (2 Cor. 4:8–9). This is the miracle of the hope of Christ in our hearts. It strengthens us in the middle of the suffering and the mystery. It keeps us from giving in to disappointment, from losing heart, so that "though our outer man is decaying, yet our inner man is being renewed day by day" (2 Cor. 4:16).

This is our new covenant reality. The Holy Spirit's love and strength, poured out in our hearts, give us the courage to hope even in the midst of an imperfect and sometimes disappointing world. And if we embrace hope, if we sing Christ's hope as our song, we will discover not just the hope that gets us through the hard places, but the hope that calls us into our destiny (see Eph. 1:18).

\*\*\*

Of course, it's so much easier to talk about this than to live it. Many of us have lived our lives in a cycle of disappointed hopes. And we know this is a painful way to live. The good news is, God has provided a better way. And if we bravely embrace the journey, he can lead us into the quality of hope that cannot be disappointed, the quality of faith that cannot be offended, the quality of love that looks like Jesus. It is not an easy or painless journey, but it is our calling. On that narrow path, we are transformed into the mighty children of God, the new creation in Christ, and we are empowered to fulfill our destiny.

On that path, we become the people with faith, hope, and love mighty enough to not just endure the storm, but to find heaven's solution for it.

When Jesus fell asleep in the middle of a storm, his disciples got angry at him, saying "Teacher, do You not care that we are perishing?" (Mark 4:38). Their fear got the best of them, and they doubted his goodness. But after Jesus calmed the storm, he rebuked his disciples: "Why are you afraid? Do you still have no faith?" (Mark 4:40). Matthew recorded Jesus as saying, "Why are you afraid, you men of little faith?" (Matt. 8:26). And in Luke, he said simply, "Where is your faith?" (Luke 8:25).

I always wondered about this story—wondered why Jesus would rebuke his disciples so harshly for being afraid in a real-life storm that could have killed them. After all, they woke him up because they believed he could do something about it. Doesn't that show their faith? But then I heard a preacher suggest an alternate reading—that perhaps Jesus' frustration with the disciples stemmed from their failure to live out what he had just taught them. In both Mark and Luke, this story of the storm is preceded by several of Jesus' parables about the kingdom. And Mark tells us, "He did not speak to them [the people] without a parable; but He was explaining everything privately to His own disciples" (Mark 4:34).

Jesus' disciples got the inside story, the special briefings, the top-tier training. Jesus was strategically equipping them to carry the kingdom forward on earth after he left, and as we see throughout the New Testament, miracles and supernatural power were a big part of that role. Of all the people Jesus had taught and ministered to thus far, his disciples were the ones most likely to be able to demonstrate kingdom power. Perhaps when the waves began to billow and roll, Jesus thought this storm might be a good opportunity for the disciples to try out their new spiritual wings. Perhaps, like a good mother eagle, he was pushing them out of the nest to see if they would fly. Perhaps he purposely fell asleep and remained asleep during the terrifying assault of wind and waves because he wanted *them* to calm the storm.

This story challenges me, because it reminds me that Jesus' ultimate goal for my journey is bigger than my own healing. He cares deeply for each one of us, and he is so patient with us in our moments of weakness and doubt. But the story doesn't stop there. When the disciples responded in fear and doubt, Jesus still rescued them. He was patient with their process, but he also never forgot the endgame—that they would become like him. That they would do the same miracles he had done—and even greater miracles (see John 14:12).

In the apostle John's first letter, in the middle of his discussion of the power of Christ's love in us—how it makes us confident and fearless—he says, "Because as He is, so also are we in this world" (1 John 4:17). John lived through that storm. He saw Jesus calm the waves, and he heard his rebuke. John knew the power of Christ's love at work in our lives—that it could make us like him. And the hope of this "like him" was what John fixed his heart on and pointed his life toward (see 1 John 3:2–3).

Jesus' endgame for us is not the salvation prayer. He doesn't just rescue us out of darkness. He also brings us "into His marvelous light" so that we can proclaim his glory and expand the kingdom until his return (1 Pet. 2:9). Throughout the New Testament we read exhortations about growing up in Christ, becoming those who live out the gospel with power, those who demonstrate His victory regardless of circumstances. Our story is not just one of freedom and healing, but also of empowerment, so that we will become the mighty sons and daughters of God.

In his kindness, Jesus does not grow weary of our journey, and he doesn't judge us for where we are—but at the same time, he is working toward the full manifestation of his might in our lives.

This is what the battle for hope—as the answer to disappointment in our lives—is all about. Jesus' work in our lives is not just so that we find healing for the hurts of life. (Even though that is very important.) It's not even just so that we learn to live through the storms with unshakable faith. (This is also very important.) His "what's possible" for us is even greater. He died to give us the ability to learn how to step into the kingdom wisdom and resources and might needed to find solutions. To raise the dead. To silence the storms.

To do this, we need to stop living like Elisha's servant and begin living like Elisha, the miracle-worker. Like many of us, Elisha's servant looked to his surroundings to determine his hope. When he arose one morning to find their city surrounded by an enemy army of horses and chariots, he was struck with fear. "Alas, my master! What shall we do?" (2 Kings 6:15). He saw no hope, no way out from the plots of their enemies.

But Elisha told him, "Do not fear, for those who are with us are more than those who are with them" (2 Kings 6:16). Then, Elisha prayed that God would open the eyes of his servant so that he could see in the spirit—so that he could see with the eyes of hope. When the servant's eyes were opened, he saw "the mountain was full of horses and chariots of fire all around Elisha" (2 Kings 6:17). This is the journey God wants to take us on, so that we can see with heaven's eyes, so that our hope will be firmly fixed on heaven's realities.

This kind of hope will become an inextinguishable fire within us. It will be a love song and a mighty sword. It will be Christ in us, the hope of glory (see Col. 1:27).

***

Just as healing from disappointment and loss is not a formula, but a journey, so too, the way back to hope is an individualized path we walk with God. Yet, the Bible also gives us several signposts to guide our journey out of disappointment and into the fearless hope of Christ.

The first of these signposts is found in Paul's words to the church at Rome: "Now may the God of hope fill you with all joy and peace in believing, so that you will abound in hope by the power of the Holy Spirit" (Rom. 15:13). Here, God calls himself the God of hope. It's one of the ways he names or defines himself. He delights in bringing hope into people's lives. He has never experienced hopelessness. He has never looked at our lives and felt despair. Instead, he has sent the Holy Spirit to help us abound— overflow—in hope. This happens as we are filled "with all joy and peace in believing." Hope is the outworking of God's joy and peace in our lives as we choose to trust and believe in him. As we choose to trust God, he fills us with his peace and joy. The result is hope.

In other words, hope is a choice.

Paul even included hope in a list of instructions, telling believers to rejoice in hope (see Rom. 12:10–13). Hope, like each of the instructions Paul gave, involves an action we decide to take—or not take. And in this specific context, Paul's exhortation—"rejoicing in hope, persevering in tribulation, devoted to prayer"—has to do with trusting in God's ability to bring justice on our behalf. This kind of hope is a fierce decision we make and a weapon against the darkness.

So often we think of hope as an emotion, and it is true that we can feel hopeful. But heavenly hope—like forgiveness—is a decision we make based on our faith in the goodness of God. I have felt this so clearly in the seasons of walking through the valley of the shadow of death. Hope and despair were clearly before me, and I had to choose. And when I chose hope, it wasn't because I had magnificent faith, but because I had enough faith to not give up. It was because I decided that no matter what—no matter how hopeless it seemed—I would keep believing. I must keep believing. And always, Jesus has met me in that place and shown himself faithful.

The second signpost for hope is also found in Paul's letter to the church in Rome:

> For in hope we have been saved, but hope that is seen is not hope; for who hopes for what he already

sees? But if we hope for what we do not see, with perseverance we wait eagerly for it (Romans 8:24–25).

Because hope is in the unseen, it is always a risk. I've heard hope defined as "the confident expectation of good."[19] We could call it kingdom expectancy—a belief that the kingdom of God is always expanding and that we can expect to see God's goodness in our lives. If faith is "the assurance of things hoped for, the conviction of things not seen" (Heb 11:1), then hope is the outworking of faith.

In other words, if hope is a choice that demands risk, then ultimately, the way back to hope is a road that is always before us. It is always available. Whether we step onto it is up to us. We get to choose to trust and hope again. We get to risk it all on the narrow path (see Matt. 7:13–14). And if we do, we will find Jesus deeply invested and present in our journey, giving us eyes to see and believe for the next step again and again and again. Teaching us to step into a hope that won't give up, a hope that stills the storm.

This is most true in the moments when hope seems impossible. When, like Paul, we feel the sentence of death within ourselves (see 2 Cor. 1:8–10). When, like Abraham, "in hope against hope," we believe (see Rom. 4:18). When, like the woman with the issue of blood, we risk all to grab ahold of Jesus.

This woman had just as much reason as the man at the pool of Bethesda to lose hope and give in to disappointment. She had been hemorrhaging blood for twelve years, and although she had sought advice from many doctors, no one could help her (see Luke 8:43–48). This ailment would be hard to deal with today; I cannot imagine how horrifying it was back then. Not only did they have fewer options for how to manage such a problem, medically and sanitarily, but the Jews also had strict laws about purity that labeled anyone who was bleeding as unclean. She would have been isolated from people almost entirely.

Twelve years is a long time to be alone and hurting. Twelve years is a long time to keep hoping that something might change, that God would rescue her. Yet somehow she did.

I know what it's like to grow weary in waiting for a miracle. I'm still waiting for a miracle in the nerves in my wrists, arms, neck, and shoulders. I've found a laser therapy that has helped significantly, but it probably will not resolve the issue completely. I still need a miracle. I have received prayer many times from many different people. Sometimes, I've felt certain my miracle would come. But so far, that miracle has not made itself known in my body.

And every time I have the opportunity to receive prayer, I have a choice to make. Will I choose hope and faith? Will I receive prayer again—like it's the first time—with confident expectation of good in my heart? Or will I listen to disappointment? Every time, disappointment whispers in my ears, telling me it's no use. At times, I have listened to that voice. I have chosen not to receive prayer. Or I've received it reluctantly, because others wanted to pray, and I felt bad turning them down.

But then I felt God convict me. *That's no way to live,* he said. *Don't shut your heart off from hope. Stay fierce. Keep believing. I am here with you, and I am your healer.*

And I try to imagine what the woman with the issue of blood first thought when she heard about Jesus. Did she wrestle with whether to seek him out? Did she fear what might not happen? What we do know is that, regardless of any inner turmoil, she left her isolation. She broke all the rules, entering into a great throng of people, wrestling through the crowd in order to get near to Jesus.

She risked everything on hope.

And when she finally touched him, she found the tree of life.

# ENDNOTES

1. Ann Voskamp, "How Real People Make (Real) Love," February 13, 2020; annvoskamp.com (accessed January 2022). Since the writing of my first draft, Ann Voskamp's blog post has been revised to reflect the focus of her new book, *Waymaker,* and it no longer contains the material I reference here.

2. C. S. Lewis, *The Four Loves* (New York: HarperOne, 1960), 155–156.

3. J. R. R. Tolkein, *The Return of the King* (New York: Ballantine Books, 1955), 290.

4. Nora McInerny, "We Don't 'Move On' from Grief We Move Forward with It," *TEDWomen 2018;* www.ted.com (accessed January 11, 2022).

5. Michael S. Heiser, *The Unseen Realm* (Bellingham, WA: Lexham Press, 2015), 66.

6. I first heard this interpretation of this passage in a sermon by Bill Johnson titled, "How to Overcome Disappointment." It is available at shop.bethel.com.

7. N. T. Wright, "Matthew 15.21-28 The Canaanite Woman," *Matthew for Everyone, Part I* (London, UK & Louisville, KY: The Society for Promoting Christian Knowledge & Westminster John Knox Press: 2004), 200.

8. For a great discussion on the question of whether God is capricious and uncaring, see *Is God a Moral Monster* by Paul Copan (Baker Books, 2011).

9. N. T. Wright, "Matthew 15.21-28 The Canaanite Woman," *Matthew for Everyone, Part I* (London, UK & Louisville, KY: The Society for Promoting Christian Knowledge & Westminster John Knox Press: 2004), 201.

10. Madeline L'Engle, *A Circle of Quiet* (New York: Harper Collins, 1972), 243.

11. For more on declarations, I recommend the materials of Steve and Wendy Backlund. www.ignitinghope.com.

12. Foster Cline and Jim Fay, *Parenting with Love and Logic* (Colorado Springs, CO: NavPress, 2006), 145.

13. *Ibid.*, 146.

14. For more on healthy boundaries and confrontation, I recommend *Keep Your Love On* by Danny Silk.

15. W. H. Auden, "Musée des Beaux Arts," ll. 3–5.

16. Emily Dickinson, "'Hope' is the thing with feathers," public domain, ll. 1–4.

17. *Ibid.*, ll. 6–7.

18. I first heard this interpretation of this passage in a sermon by Bill Johnson titled, "How to Overcome Disappointment." It is available at shop.bethel.com.

19. This phrase was coined by Steve and Wendy Backlund. www.ignitinghope.com.

# ABOUT THE AUTHOR

AMY CALKINS IS A freelance writer and editor, a published poet, a former pastor, and a homeschool mom. Over the last fifteen years, Amy has edited hundreds of books for a variety of publishers and authors, as well as ghostwritten seven nonfiction books. Her poems have also been published in several literary journals and anthologies.

Alongside her editing and writing work, Amy gives much of her time to homeschooling her four children, ages seven through fifteen. She and her husband of sixteen years, Mark, also serve on a volunteer basis at their home church.

In her free time, Amy enjoys reading literature, theology and poetry, playing board and card games with her family, watching terrific movies, and having deep conversations with friends over a good London Fog. Amy, Mark, and their kids live in Lancaster County, PA.

You can connect with Amy on Facebook or Instagram @amycalkinswrites or at amycalkins.com.

www.ingramcontent.com/pod-product-compliance
Lightning Source LLC
Chambersburg PA
CBHW020401130626
46549CB00006B/2386